BANKING ON CLOUD DATA PLATFORMS:
A GUIDE

DILLIP KUMAR
SARAH MOHAPATRA

BLUEROSE PUBLISHERS
India | U.K.

Copyright © Dillip Kumar, Sarah Mohapatra 2023

All rights reserved by author. No part of this publication may be reproduced, stored in a retrieval system or transmitted in any form or by any means, electronic, mechanical, photocopying, recording or otherwise, without the prior permission of the author. Although every precaution has been taken to verify the accuracy of the information contained herein, the publisher assume no responsibility for any errors or omissions. No liability is assumed for damages that may result from the use of information contained within.

BlueRose Publishers takes no responsibility for any damages, losses, or liabilities that may arise from the use or misuse of the information, products, or services provided in this publication.

For permissions requests or inquiries regarding this publication,
please contact:

BLUEROSE PUBLISHERS
www.BlueRoseONE.com
info@bluerosepublishers.com
+91 8882 898 898
+4407342408967

ISBN: 978-93-5819-819-5

Cover design: Tahira
Typesetting: Tanya Raj Upadhyay

First Edition: October 2023

Foreword

"Marketing Myopia" is the quintessential big hit HBR piece in 1960. In it, Theodore Levitt, who was then a lecturer in business administration at the Harvard Business School, introduced the famous question, "What business are you really in?" and the claim that, the railroad executives saw themselves as being in the transportation business rather than the railroad business, The railroads did not stop growing because the need for passenger and freight transportation declined. Because that need was filled by others (cars, Trucks, Airplanes, and even telephones) instead of transportation oriented; they were product oriented instead of customer oriented. Hollywood narrowly evaded complete domination by television. Amazon inaugurates its Go store in New York. The Dubai Formula One Race is a fiercely competitive event where data analysis plays a pivotal role in achieving victory. Walmart has introduced its 'Last Mile' strategy to outpace Amazon's delivery prowess. While discussing these various business cases, the underlying principle remains clear: making data-driven decisions is essential for survival and progress.

For as long as we've been talking about Data and Service, something inside data is a powerhouse. In fact, before we even had the word Data and Cloud in our lexicon, back when it was just good old-fashioned spreadsheet driven Data movement, now we were talking about data: how to access it, where it lives, who "owns" it. Data is all-important—vital for the continued success of our business—but has also been seen as a massive constraint in how we design and evolve our systems. My own journey into Data Analytics began with work I was doing to help organizations build software sitting on mammoth of Data. This meant a lot of time was spent on things like cycle time analysis, build pipeline design, test automation, infrastructure automation and Data Validation etc. The advent of the cloud was a huge boon to the work we were doing, as the improved automation made us even more productive. But

I kept hitting some fundamental issues. All too often, the software wasn't designed in a way that made it easy to ship. And data was at the heart of the problem. Back then, the most common pattern I saw for service-based systems was sharing a database among multiple services. The rationale was simple: the data I need is already in this other database, and accessing a database is easy, so I'll just reach in and grab what I need. This may allow for fast development of a new service, but over time it becomes a major constraint.

A shared database creates a huge coupling point in your architecture. It becomes difficult to understand what changes can be made to a schema shared by multiple services. David Parnas showed us back in 1971 that the secret to creating software whose parts could be changed independently was to hide information between modules. But at a swoop, exposing a schema to multiple services prohibits our ability to independently evolve our codebases.

As the needs and expectations of software changed, IT organizations changed with them. The shift from siloed IT toward business- or product-aligned teams helped improve the customer focus of those teams. This shift often happened in concert with the move to improve the autonomy of those teams, allowing them to develop new ideas, implement them, and then ship them, all while reducing the need for coordination with other parts of the organization. But highly coupled architectures require heavy coordination between systems and the teams that maintain them—they are the enemy of any organization that wants to optimize autonomy. Amazon spotted this many years ago. It wanted to improve team autonomy to allow the company to evolve and ship software more quickly, Attached data piece with this software as part of ingredient.

To achieve this objective, Amazon established small, autonomous teams responsible for the entire delivery lifecycle. After leaving Amazon for Google, Steve Yegge made an infamous attempt to encapsulate what made these teams highly effective in his widely discussed 'Platform Rant.' In this piece, he articulated Amazon CEO Jeff Bezos's directives on team collaboration and system design. These specific points particularly resonate with me: 1) All teams are now required to expose their data and functionality through service interfaces. 2) Teams are mandated to communicate exclusively through these interfaces. 3) No other forms of inter-process communication are permitted: no direct linking, no direct access to another team's data store, no shared-memory models, no unauthorized access points. The sole permissible means of communication is through service interface calls over the network, often employed to resolve data discrepancies across disparate systems. The questions surrounding diverse data types, substantial data volumes, and strategies for monetization continually intrigue me.

Clearly defined interfaces play a crucial role, as does the concept of data encapsulation. When data storage becomes necessary, it should ideally be encapsulated within a specific service rather than being directly accessible by other services. A robustly defined interface should dictate the terms for accessing and manipulating this data. Much of my recent years have revolved around advocating for this concept. While there's growing recognition of its importance, challenges persist. The fact remains that services must collaborate and occasionally share data. The question is, how can this be accomplished effectively? How can it be done in a manner that aligns with the latency and load considerations of your application? What strategies should be employed when one service requires substantial data from another? As the volume of data from various source systems grows, how can integration be harmonized to ensure uniform access, facilitate controlled processing, cleansing, and secure storage? And ultimately, how can multiple systems make the most of this data?

The fundamental principle of platforms, often articulated as 'Eat Your Own Dog Food,' can also be reframed as 'Commence with a Platform, and Make It the Foundation for All.' The notion of simply adding it on later is not a viable approach, especially not without significant challenges. Just ask those who've been involved in the intricate process of platforming software giants like MS Office or Amazon. Delaying this foundational step can result in a tenfold increase in effort compared to getting it right from the start. Shortcuts are not permissible; there can be no clandestine pathways granting special priority access to internal applications, under any circumstances. Instead, the focus should be on preemptively addressing the most complex issues. In an era where data volume and scope have surged exponentially, the imperative is to construct a data platform that boasts scalability, resilience, and universal accessibility. This underscores the critical question for technocrats: how to construct a Data Platform that mirrors the success of application development platforms.

Larry Tesler may have convinced Bezos that he was no Steve Jobs, but Bezos realized that he didn't need to be Steve Jobs in order to provide everyone with the right products: interfaces and workflows that they liked and felt at ease with. He just needed to enable third-party developers to do it, and it would happen automatically.

I extend my apologies to those among you (which is quite a few) for whom the points I'm making might seem exceedingly self-evident, because indeed, they are glaringly so. However, despite their inherent clarity, we often fall short in their application. We seem to have a limited grasp of the concepts of Platforms and Accessibility, even though, in essence, they are intertwined. Platforms, in fact, are the solution to achieving broad accessibility. In simpler terms, a platform embodies the very essence of accessibility.

I spent approximately four years at Axis Bank before joining HDFC Bank, where I've been for the past six months. What immediately caught my attention about both organizations—and a perception that's consistently reaffirmed—is their exceptional excellence. Remarkably, they each take distinct approaches, even though both banks are similarly guided by regulatory bodies. Last time I wrote an article Carbon the thrill of human on people and Macro Management.An article delving into the multifaceted human aspects and the exhilaration they bring to project management. This perspective offers deeper insights, especially when navigating the appraisal cycle amidst a comprehensive evaluation involving various stakeholders, from the board and HR to peers—akin to an alligator wrestling match

Preface

In 2006, I was employed at Daimler Chrysler in Michigan, USA. The office environment during that period was imbued with a vibrant energy, marked by a multitude of intriguing developments. My role encompassed working on Mainframe systems while also offering support for Java-based application development. The project was under the enthusiastic leadership of Mr. Michael, a dynamic and cheerful leader who infused his infectious enthusiasm into virtually every aspect of our work. The project itself constituted a fairly typical, medium-sized enterprise application

It had a web portal where customers could request a variety of conveyancing services. The system would then run various synchronous and asynchronous processes to put the myriad of services they requested into action. There were a number of interesting elements to that particular project, but the one that really stuck with me was the way the data is being served when there is a request made. While an organization has many systems to be stitched, many databases have to be plugged, high collaboration of events with many RPCs (remote procedure calls). Data Fetching and serving was tough while you have a heterogeneous system. I thought this one felt very different. There was something inherently spritely about the way you could plug new services right into different Data Systems and something deeply satisfying about tailing the log of bringing data into the user side and watching the "narrative" of the system whizz past. Initial anxieties developed on how the Complex data system will be processed, integrated and served to the customer. There are many data types, mostly Cobol VSAM files, some DB2 Databases and some Files in the FTP folder that have to be accessed, parsed with the application and rendered in the web portal. Interesting problem was to solve.

During that same year in 2006, Doug Cutting introduced the Hadoop Framework to support the Nutch Search Engine at Yahoo. It marked the first time the world was introduced to the concepts of unstructured and semi-structured data, along with methods for processing and deriving meaning from it. This technological development inspired me to delve into this emerging field. As a result, we conceptualized a product called 'iCollab,' a collaborative platform designed to enhance productivity and break down silos among vendors working within an organization. It aimed to address the absence of centralized knowledge, innovation, and collaboration, which often hindered access to critical documentation. Similar to today's Jira and Confluence in the DevOps domain, this platform goes further by offering capabilities for processing manuscripts, text, email, chat, innovation workflows, and more. It stands as an early adopter of Hadoop technology. Patent was issued based on this Product and The Data Revolution began its gradual ascent from that point onward

After a span of a few years, specifically in 2017, I was working at a prominent financial institution situated in London, UK. During this time, the institution embarked on an ambitious project: the establishment of a Cloud Platform. The primary objective was to seamlessly migrate a substantial volume of data, exceeding 25 petabytes, from an on-premises Hadoop infrastructure and the core operational system to the cloud. One significant challenge we encountered in this undertaking revolved around effectively managing cryptographic keys and establishing a secure private vault to safeguard sensitive information. During this phase, I participated in an event attended by over 300 bankers, along with representatives from Google, AWS, and Azure, focusing on Data and Cloud in Canary Wharf, London. Many investment banks shared common concerns and we're striving to formulate cloud architectures, roadmaps, and bulletproof strategies to address critical aspects like PII, SPDI, GDPR compliance, and more in the cloud. This marked an incredible beginning for the era of cloud computing in the realm of data. The datasets that banks handle, including trades, valuations, references, CRM, and hedging, are akin to their lifeblood. The ability to ingest, process, and provide these datasets as data services with robust security measures lies at the core of every bank's operation.

I find this sort of problem quite compelling: it was technically challenging and, although a number of banks and other large companies had thought of implementing Cloud, it felt like the technology had moved on to a point where we could build something really interesting and transformative. So, it slowly became apparent that, for all its features—the data-driven precaching that made joins fast, the SQL-over Document interface, the immutable data model, and late-bound schema—what most customers needed was really subtly different, and somewhat simpler.

In May 2023, while I was speaking at the Gartner forum in Mumbai, India, I came to realize that numerous talented individuals worldwide had developed numerous data analytics platforms, and this space was continuously expanding. However, a critical challenge emerged: connecting all these developments and creating knowledge that could be comprehensively understood and readily implemented. It was during this time that the idea of writing a book to document this journey and address the concept of 'Data Myopia' arose. Ms. Sarah Mohapatra, my co-author, was instrumental in encouraging and contributing to this endeavor, particularly in the realm of cloud use cases.

Acknowledgments:

Many people contributed to this book, both directly and indirectly, but a special thanks to Avinash Raghavendra, Pinaki Halder and of course my ever-lovingly wife Dipti, Son Swaraj and My Parents Dhruba charan and late mother Badani

We would like to express our heartfelt gratitude to Blue Rose for their unwavering commitment to the art of publishing and for believing in the vision behind this book. Their expertise, dedication, and tireless efforts have transformed our manuscript into a reality that now reaches the hands of readers. This book would not have been possible without their invaluable contributions.

About Authors:

Dillip Kumar is working as Senior Vice President, at HDFC bank and heading the Data Cloud Platform along with Data engineering. Prior to this, he was heading Big Data Lake, Data function and Communication Platform in the Axis bank. He has also worked at other banks like HSBC, Deutsche in the technical leadership role where he set up Big Data, AI, Cloud Platform from scratch with PBs of Data being processed and 1000 use cases being built on the Data Platform. Dillip has spent over 25 years in the Technology industry mostly with Bank, IT Consulting, Architecture. He is also a Board Member of one startup company. He has worked for TCS, IBM and Capgemini as part of IT Consulting service and worked in many countries including USA, UK, Europe, India etc. He is an inventor of the IT Product(iCollab), Having Patent and open-source contributor. He is a frequent speaker at industry conferences including Gartner and other CIO Forums He is an author of Book, Article and Magazine on BFSI. Dillip holds An MBA from IIM Kolkata and Bachelor in Engineering from NIT, Rourkela, India

Sarah Mohapatra is a high school student currently in the 12th grade. She wears many hats, including being the founder of SH2 (Share Hope and Healing), A youth based initiative that focuses on addressing mental challenges faced by teenagers during their educational journey and aspirations for their future careers. She is holding the position of social media Director at WFS, she is an avid enthusiast of cutting-edge technologies like Cloud Computing, AI, Blockchain, and the Metaverse. Notably, she's a passionate developer with a knack for Python programming, specializing in Cloud and AI applications. Her portfolio boasts projects developed on the Google Cloud Platform (GCP) and Blockchain technology. she's also an avid reader with a passion for sharing knowledge. She has written and published two articles on topics ranging from Blockchain to the Metaverse, showcasing her commitment to spreading awareness and understanding of these emerging technologies.

Evolution of Data Journey

In the 1970s, the concept of decision support systems (DSS) emerged, which focused on providing executives and managers with tools to access and analyze data for decision-making. This marked the beginning of the need for centralized data storage and analysis.

In the 1980s, companies began to build data warehouses as a central repository for storing and consolidating data from various operational systems. The purpose was to provide a single source of truth for reporting and analysis.

In 1988, Bill Inmon, often referred to as the "father of data warehousing," introduced the concept of a data warehouse as a subject-oriented, integrated, non-volatile, and time-variant collection of data. This framework laid the foundation for modern data warehousing.

In the 1990s, advancements in hardware and software technologies enabled the growth of data warehousing. Relational database management systems (RDBMS) became the primary technology for storing and managing data in data warehouses.

In 1996, Ralph Kimball, another influential figure in data warehousing, introduced the concept of dimensional modeling. Kimball's approach emphasized the use of star and snowflake schemas for designing data warehouses, which simplified querying and analysis.

During the late 1990s and early 2000s, data warehousing evolved further with the emergence of online analytical processing (OLAP) and data mining technologies. OLAP allowed for multidimensional analysis, while data mining enabled organizations to discover patterns and insights from large datasets.

In the 2004's Facebook and in the 2006's Twitter collected various types of user data, including personal information such as names, email addresses, and profile details. Additionally, they collected data on user interactions, such as posts, comments, likes, and shares and build Apis for data consumption to third party like GNIP, Board reader etc.

In the 2010s, the rise of big data presented new challenges and opportunities for data warehousing. Companies began to incorporate unstructured and semi-structured data sources into their data warehouses, alongside traditional structured data.

In the 2020's Rise of Cloud Data Platform as it provides Infrastructure as service(IaaS),Platform as Service(PaaS),Software as Service(SaaS) and often provide machine learning (ML) and artificial intelligence services, empowering developers and businesses to leverage advanced analytics, predictive modeling, and automation capabilities without the need for extensive expertise or infrastructure.

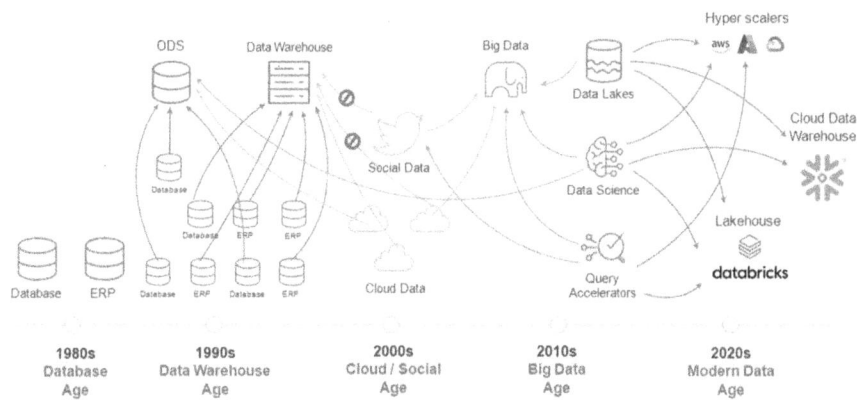

Fig 1.1: Evolution of Data Age

Table of Contents

Foreword iii

Preface vii

Acknowledgments: x

About Authors: xi

Evolution of Data Journey xii

PART 1: FIRST GENERATION 1

   Chapter 1: Data warehouse 1
      1.1 Three-Tier Architecture: 1
      1.2 Data Warehouse Models 6
      1.3 Various Uses of Data Warehouse: 11
      1.4 Architecture for Banking Data Warehouse: 30
      1.5 Source System Integration with DWH: 31
      1.6 Change Data Capture (CDC): 33
      1.7 API Integration: 36

   Chapter 2: Data Virtualization: 41

   Chapter 3: Metadata Management: 43
      3.1 Summary of First Generation 44

PART 2: SECOND GENERATION 46

   Chapter 4: Bigdata Platform 46
      4.1 What is Hadoop? 49
      4.2 Hbase –NO SQL Framework: 58

    4.3 Apache Spark – Engine replaced Hadoop Map Reduce Framework: 62

Chapter 5: Demand of Real time and Streaming: 76
    5.1 Use case for Real time 79
    5.2 Concepts of Publish/Subscribe Messaging: 80
    5.3 Kafka –Real time PubSub Messaging Platform : 83

Chapter 6: The BigSearch – Value of System records 90
    6.1 Use Cases for Search: 91
    6.2 ElasticSearch : 96
    6.3 Summary of Second Generation 102

PART 3: THIRD GENERATION 105

Chapter 7: The Cloud DataPlatform 105
    7.1 Cloud Use Cases: 106

Chapter 8: Digital Payment System 134
    8.1 Benefits of Digital Payment Systems: 134
    8.2 Payment Vision 135
    8.3 Payment Cloud Architecture 138

Chapter 9: Data Lake – One of the Complex Use case of Cloud 139
    9.1 Strategy for Cloud Platform 139
    9.2 Build the Platform : 144
    9.3 Design Consideration : 147
    9.4 Functional View of DataLake 150
    9.5 DataLake Architecture : 151

Chapter 10: The open banking transformation: 158
    10.1 The Indian Model 159
    10.2 Concern in the Open Banking: 160
    10.3 Architecture - Open Banking 162

Chapter 11: HSBC Creation of AQM using GCP 163
    11.1 Modernizing data warehousing and scaling intelligent analytics 163
    11.2 Assistance for hybrid and multi-cloud setups. 163
    11.3 Robust yet user-friendly AI and machine learning tools. 164
    11.4 Mission Critical Services 164
    11.5 Case Study 164

Chapter 12 : Data Migration from on Prem to Cloud :The Fundamentals 167
    12.1 The 4 types of cloud migration for Application : 167
    12.2 The 2 types of Cloud Migration for Data : 168

Chapter 13: Introduction to Data Mesh: 171
    13.1 Architectural failure modes of Monolithic approach : 172
    13.2 Coupled pipeline decomposition: 175
    13.3 Discoverable for Product 177
    13.4 Self-serve data platform: 181

Chapter 14 Data Security: 184
    14.1 What is Data Security? 184
    14.2 Classification of Data Security : 185
    14.3 Data Security Risks 186
    14.4 Common Data Security Solutions and Techniques 187
    14.4 Best Data Security Tips: 193
    14.5 Indian Digital Personal Data Protection Bill 2023 194
    14.6 Summary of Third Generation 197

PART 1: FIRST GENERATION

Chapter 1: Data warehouse

The fundamental idea behind a Data Warehouse is to provide a unified and reliable source of truth for a company, aiding in decision-making and predictive analysis. A Data Warehouse is an organized system that stores historical and aggregated data from one or multiple sources. It streamlines the process of generating reports and conducting analyses for organizations.

1.1 Three-Tier Architecture:

Bottom tier: The bottom tier comprises the database server, which is responsible for retrieving data from various sources, including transactional databases utilized by front-end applications.

Middle tier: The middle tier houses an OLAP server, which transforms the data into a structure better suited for analysis and complex querying. The OLAP server can work in two ways: either as an extended relational database management system that maps the operations on multidimensional data to standard relational operations (Relational OLAP), or using a multidimensional OLAP model that directly implements the multidimensional data and operations.

Top tier: The top tier is the client layer. This tier holds the tools used for high-level data analysis, querying reporting, and data mining

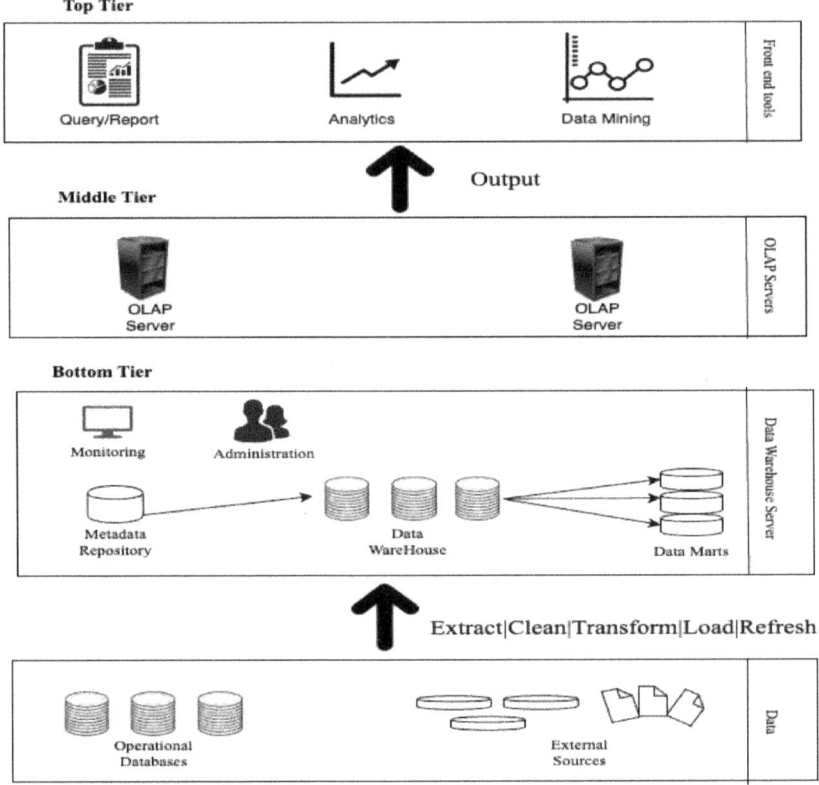

Fig 1.2: Three-tier Architecture of Data Warehouse

Two Models inspire most to DWH - Kimball vs. Inmon

Ralph Kimball's methodology places a strong emphasis on the significance of data marts, which serve as dedicated repositories for data pertaining to specific lines of business within an organization. In this framework, the data warehouse essentially functions as an amalgamation of various data marts, thereby facilitating comprehensive reporting and in-depth analysis. The Kimball approach is characterized by its **"bottom-up" orientation**, wherein data marts are initially developed and subsequently integrated into the overarching data warehouse structure.

Bill Inmon's perspective views the data warehouse as the central repository for all enterprise data. In this approach, an organization initiates the process by constructing a normalized data warehouse model, which serves as the foundation. Dimensional data marts are then derived from and aligned with this warehouse model. This methodology is commonly referred to as the **"top-down" approach** to data warehousing.

Bottom-Up Design Approach

In the context of data warehousing, the "Bottom-Up" approach entails conceptualizing a data warehouse as a specialized architecture designed for query and analytical purposes, predicated on the establishment of a star schema. This approach prioritizes the initial creation of data marts, tailored to fulfill the specific reporting and analytical requirements pertinent to distinct business processes or subject domains. Consequently, it underscores a business-centric perspective, distinguishing it from Inmon's data-centric methodology.

Data marts encompass granular transactional data, with the possibility of incorporating aggregated data as needed. Instead of adhering to the principles of normalization as seen in traditional databases, this approach espouses the utilization of denormalized dimensional databases, tailored to meet the data provisioning requisites inherent to data warehousing. Underpinning this strategy is the imperative of designing data marts with the foresight of incorporating conformed dimensions, ensuring that common entities are consistently represented across disparate data marts. These conformed dimensions serve as the linchpin that unifies the data marts into a cohesive data warehouse, frequently referred to as a virtual data warehouse.

One of the prominent advantages of the "Bottom-Up" design approach resides in its expeditious return on investment (ROI). The development of a data mart, constituting a discrete data warehouse catering to a singular subject, demands significantly less time and resources compared to the endeavor of constructing an all-encompassing enterprise-wide data warehouse. Furthermore, this methodology mitigates the risk of project failure. Inherently incremental in nature, it facilitates an adaptive learning process, enabling the project team to accumulate knowledge and expertise iteratively.

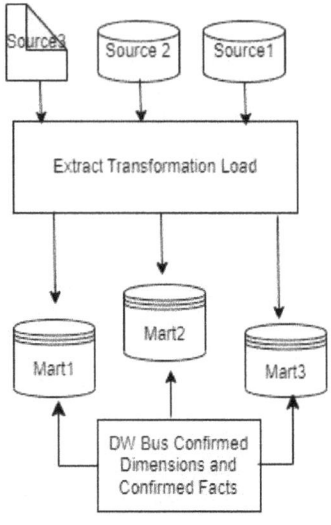

Bottom up approach(DW Bus)

Fig 1.3: Bottom-Up Approach

Advantages of the bottom-up design approach include the rapid generation of documents, flexibility in extending the data warehouse to accommodate new business units, and the straightforward process of developing new data marts and integrating them with existing ones. However, a notable disadvantage lies in the reversal of the traditional locations of the data warehouse and data marts in the bottom-up approach design.

Top-down Design Approach

In the "Top-Down" design approach, a data warehouse is delineated as a subject-oriented, time-variant, non-volatile, and integrated data repository encompassing enterprise-wide data originating from diverse sources. This data undergoes validation, reformatting, and is stored in a normalized database, adhering to third normal form (3NF) principles, serving as the foundational structure of the data warehouse. This repository contains "atomic" information, representing data at its most granular level, forming the basis from which dimensional data marts can be constructed, selectively extracting data pertinent to specific business subjects or departmental requirements. This approach is characterized as data-driven, emphasizing the initial consolidation and integration of data before formulating business-specific prerequisites for constructing data marts. Notably, this method confers the advantage of fostering a singular, integrated data source, ensuring consistency in data marts derived from it, particularly when areas of overlap exist.

Advantages of the top-down design approach encompass the streamlined loading of Data Marts directly from the central data warehouse, simplifying the process of creating new data marts. However, this method exhibits inflexibility when it comes to accommodating evolving departmental requirements and often incurs high implementation costs.

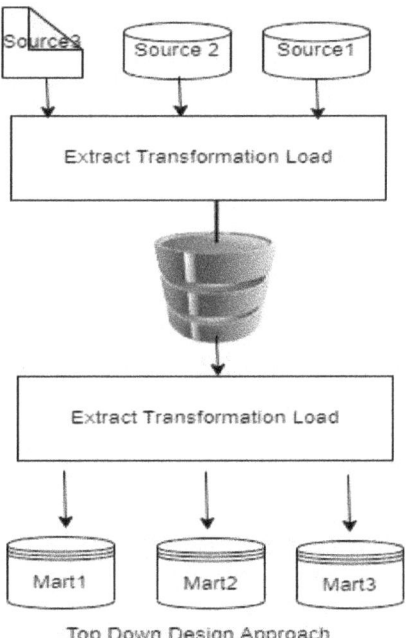

Fig 1.4: Top-down Approach

1.2 Data Warehouse Models

A virtual data warehouse is a collection of distinct databases that can be seamlessly queried together, offering users the ability to access all data as if it were consolidated into a single data warehouse. Conversely, a data mart model is employed for business-focused reporting and analysis. In this data warehousing model, data is aggregated from various source systems that pertain specifically to a particular business domain, such as sales or finance. In contrast, the enterprise data warehouse model prescribes that the data warehouse should contain aggregated data spanning the entire organization. This model envisions the data warehouse as the central hub of the enterprise's information system, housing integrated data originating from all business units.

Data Modelling Life Cycle:

It is a straightforward process of transforming the business requirements to fulfill the goals for storing, maintaining, and accessing the data within IT systems. The result is a logical and physical data model for an enterprise data warehouse.

The objective of the data modeling life cycle is primarily the creation of a storage area for business information. That area comes from the logical and physical data modeling stages

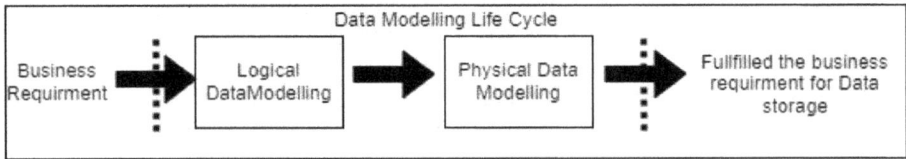

Fig 1.5: Data Modeling Life Cycle

Conceptual Data Model:

A conceptual data model recognizes the highest-level relationships between the different entities. Characteristics of the conceptual data model as below:

- It contains the essential entities and the relationships among them.
- No attribute is specified.
- No primary key is specified.

We can see that the only data shown via the conceptual data model is the entities that define the data and the relationships between those entities. No other data, as shown through the conceptual data model.

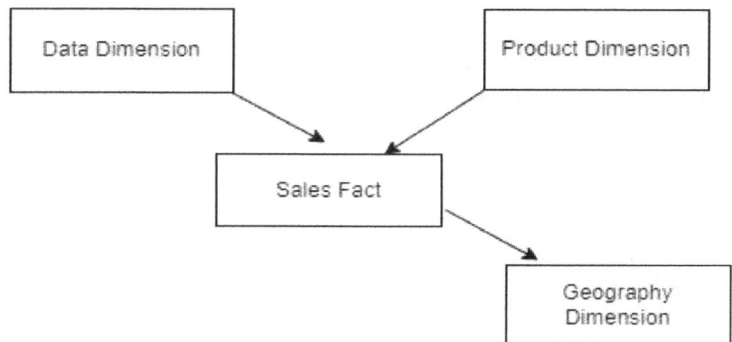

Fig 1.6: Example of Conceptual Data Model

Logical Data Model:

A logical data model outlines information structures comprehensively, without consideration for their physical database implementation. Its main goal is to document business data structures, processes, rules, and relationships within a unified logical data model view.

Features of a logical data model include:

- It involves all entities and relationships among them.
- All attributes for each entity are specified.
- The primary key for each entity is stated.
- Referential Integrity is specified (FK Relation).
- Specify primary keys for all entities.
- List the relationships between different entities.

- List all attributes for each entity.
- Normalization.
- No data types are listed

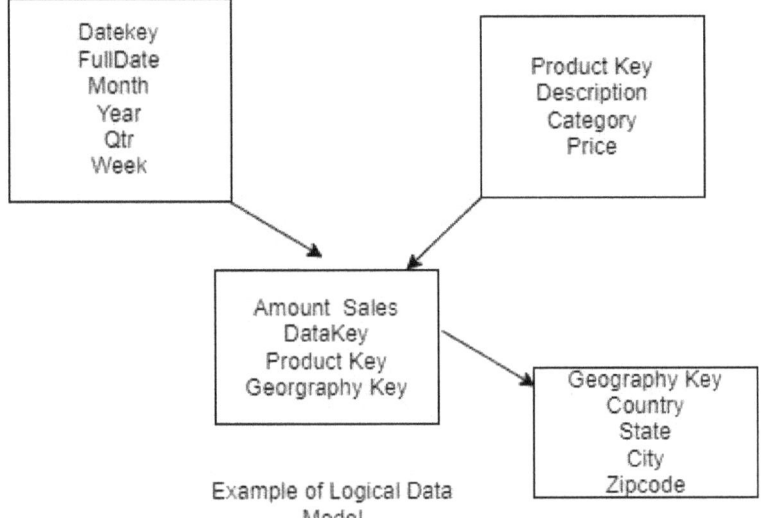

Example of Logical Data Model

Fig 1.7: Example of Logic Data Model

Physical Data Model

A physical data model details the database's presentation, including table structures, column names, data types, constraints, primary keys, foreign keys, and table relationships. Its purpose is to map the logical data model to the physical structures of the hosting RDBMS system in a data warehouse, encompassing the definition of physical RDBMS structures like tables and data types for data storage, and potentially introducing new data structures to improve query performance.

- Characteristics of a physical data model
- Specification all tables and columns.
- Foreign keys are used to recognize relationships between tables.
- The steps for physical data model design which are as follows:

- Convert entities to tables.
- Convert relationships to foreign keys.
- Convert attributes to columns.

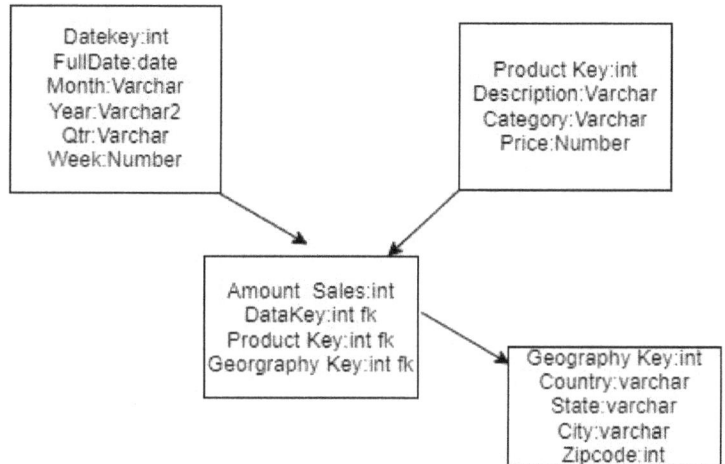

Fig 1.8: Example of Physical Model

Star Schema vs. Snowflake Schema

The star schema and snowflake schema are two ways to structure the data in the data warehouse.

The star schema has a centralized data repository, stored in a fact table. The schema splits the fact table into a series of denormalized dimension tables. The fact table contains aggregated data to be used for reporting purposes while the dimension table describes the stored data.

Denormalized designs are less complex because the data is grouped. The fact table uses only one link to join to each dimension table. The star schema's simpler design makes it much easier to write complex queries.

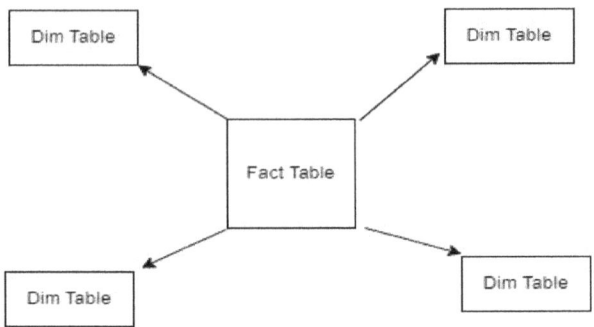

Fig 1.9: Star Schema

The snowflake schema is different because it normalizes the data. Normalization means efficiently organizing the data so that all data dependencies are defined, and each table contains minimal redundancies. Single dimension tables thus branch out into separate dimension tables.

The snowflake schema uses less disk space and better preserves data integrity. The main disadvantage is the complexity of queries required to access data—each query must dig deep to get to the relevant data because there are multiple joins.

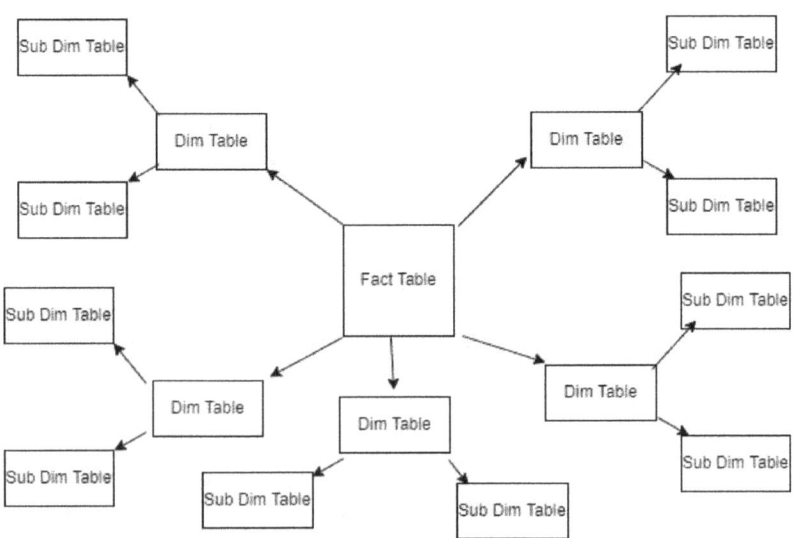

Fig 1.10: Snowflake Schema

1.3 Various Uses of Data Warehouse:

Risk Management and Compliance:

As the money movers, both corporate and personal, banks hold enormous sway over the economic environment. However, that power is often wielded irresponsibly as financial professionals cling to their outdated manual processes to complete their period end. Regulatory compliance and financial risk are ever-present and ever-changing threats within banking and finance, and these employees must have a dependable process in order to avoid costly and embarrassing misstatements.

As you're probably well aware, the U.S. federal government, responding to past negative economic ramifications, imposed a series of regulatory standards that affected banks above a certain asset threshold. Known as the Dodd-Frank Wall Street Reform and Consumer Protection Act, these standards have been in place since 2010.

Recently, that threshold was raised, though with a small modification. Specifically, the 'Bank SIFI' threshold of the Dodd-Frank act was raised from $50 to $250 billion.

The amendment comes with the caveat that the Federal Reserve retains the discretion to apply enhanced regulatory standards to any specific bank greater than $100 billion.

While the amendment ostensibly gave banks a bit more leeway as they grow, it also presents a new threat connected to risk and compliance in banking. Banks can now grow to reach greater heights unencumbered by regulation, but with a looming axe waiting to fall. It is imperative that you are committed to your compliance process and stay aware of what's to come if you want to be prepared for future growth. To guide you, we have identified three best practices for risk and compliance in the banking industry.

Truth through Technology

The first step in risk management is being prepared with the proper tools that will allow you to effectively combat financial risk for compliance in banking. As companies prepare for and handle growing levels of financial scrutiny and overall growth within the company, it's important that modern problems have modern solutions. Indeed, more than 40% of North American banks have dedicated more than 25% of their IT budget to update outdated legacy systems2.

Any institution that plans to scale up needs to have the means to efficiently complete their reconciliations, monitor their task lists and establish risk management controls throughout the entire process – this cannot be done when manually maintained spreadsheets are involved in any point of the process. Fortunately, improving banking technology benefits not only the organization but customers too. Process improvements on the backend can provide customers with better financial protections at the user level. Also, the larger your customer base becomes, the more efficient your technology-based processes will need to be.

Control Your Compliance

Because regulation enforcement can be imposed below the official threshold, it pays to be prepared. And, in an attempt to do just that, according to an American Banker Association (ABA) survey, 75% of community banks have had to hire additional staff to cope with new regulations3. However, throwing people at the problem can actually increase the chance of error because you're essentially compounding the risk of data-entry mistakes during the reconciliation and entire financial close process. Manual spreadsheets do not provide sufficient visibility to all the possible instances of error and their sources.

In order to stay competitive, you must accelerate data-driven business decisions with real-time information through an improved financial close process. In such tools, risk-based alerts allow you to respond and correct issues before they rise to the level of outside scrutiny. Your organization would be able to thrive, safely without necessarily needing to hire additional staff.

Business Intelligence and Reporting:

The value of business intelligence reporting lies in its ability to provide an in-depth understanding of a company's performance and operations that can be acted upon. In traditional, more legacy analytics practices, business intelligence reports are prepared in advance by highly technical teams for executives. By providing accurate and timely insights into trends, customer preferences, market conditions, and more, BI reporting helps executives make smarter decisions that can improve the overall efficiency and effectiveness of their business. In addition to helping with decision-making, BI reporting also helps businesses identify new opportunities for growth and improvement.

In today's world, however, many companies have adopted an entirely new business intelligence strategy, where users of all skills can engage with data. As part of these efforts, they've implemented ad hoc analysis and reporting to scale the impact of their data. These kinds of tools allow business users to ask and answer questions on their own as the need arises, turn those questions into interactive data visualizations and reports, and share these instantly with others in their organization.

Here are the primary business intelligence reporting capabilities and use cases

Self-service BI enables users to easily analyze data without writing code. Further, modern BI platforms that use an associative engine allow users to explore data freely in any direction, recalculating analytics and highlighting data relationships after each click.

Dashboards and data visualization are used to improve understanding, allow collaboration and share information across an organization. Interactive dashboards that include rich data visualizations of charts, graphs and maps make it easier for stakeholders to understand and collaborate. Modern BI tools make it simple for any user to easily interact with the data themselves and create their own custom dashboards with drag-and-drop tools.

Static reports and alerting are also important ways for stakeholders to stay on top of their business and take quick action. BI software should allow users to easily build and share static reports in popular document formats and to set up data-driven, real-time alerts when KPIs pass a threshold.

Augmented analytics uses artificial intelligence (AI) and machine learning to enhance human intuition with suggested insights and analyses, automation of tasks, search & natural language interaction, and real-time advanced analytics

Embedded BI integrates business intelligence capabilities within applications, products, portals or processes. This lets employees, partners, customers and suppliers quickly access data and insights in their workflows rather than switching to a separate application. In this way, embedded BI helps people find insights and make better decisions faster

Mobile BI means that users can share their insights and collaborate with other stakeholders on any device, even if they're offline. Given the way work happens today, users need to be able to access and analyze their data wherever they are

Product and Service Innovation: In the decades before the Great Recession, banks relied on unrelenting product innovation to drive growth. From reward cards and no-fee checking to adjustable-rate mortgages, debit cards and instant credit, this innovation has benefitted customers and banks alike.

But over the last two decades, banks have shifted their focus away from innovation. The 2008 financial crisis turned the attention of banks toward economic recovery, adhering to new regulatory standards and driving down costs by digitizing their processes and experiences.

In parallel, changes in consumer needs and the rise of new technologies set the stage for a new operating environment. But innovation did not slow down. Neobanks, fintechs and bigtechs started driving industry innovations such as buy now, pay later lending models and early payday lending.

Today, new competitive threats continue to emerge in all shapes and sizes. Bigtechs are leveraging their consumer data, advanced analytics capabilities and large network effects to partner with nimble fintechs, capturing significant market share across their expanding global footprint—all without a banking license. These non-traditional competitors show ambitions beyond becoming digital banks, and their foray into financial services focuses on creating new sources of value and strengthening their ecosystem by reimagining business models.

What impact have zero rates had on banking product innovation?

A decade of zero rates distorted the market by causing a flood of cheap cash and enabling alternative lenders and venture-capital-backed fintechs to fuel the acquisition of emerging and underserved customer segments. During this period, the product calculus changed rapidly, forcing banks to focus on optimizing and marketing individual products rather than developing integrated propositions for customers.

This is revealed in the shrinking role of banks relative to the overall financial system, new competitors and other intermediaries. This trend is apparent in developed economies such as the US, the UK, Europe, Japan and others. This has been partly engineered by regulators seeking to reduce risk within the banking system that became evident in the 2008 financial crisis.

While these regulations and risk controls aimed to build a more resilient economy, the legal, regulatory and policy standards have not evolved to address the new competitive banking environment. The last decade saw an explosion of non-regulated players, such as fintechs, bigtechs and non-banks, and these competitors have attacked the banking value chain to build and serve all the products of a bank without the constraints of banking regulations.

Additionally, during this time, the persistence of zero interest rates resulted in four major directional changes that drove customers and growth outside the banking industry:

The rise of neobanks

Personal banking experienced a proliferation of new fintech banks, reaching 250 globally in 2022. Cheap deposits and streamlined experiences powered by more than $300bn in funding helped neobanks open more than 33mn accounts since 2019.

The explosion of digital lending

Rock-bottom rates fueled massive off-balance-sheet funding. The number of personal and consumer lenders exploded, while new entrants such as neobanks quintupled the value of digital lending since 2010. (Even Goldman got into the game with Marcus offering personal loans and savings.)

The disaggregation of SMB products

Fintechs systematically disaggregated small business banking, with entrants like Square and Kabbage emerging. PayPal acquired Swift Financial to bolster its SMB lending business. Brex built a SMB credit card business. And Shopify and Uber started offering integrated banking.

The replacement of banks by private equity (PE) firms

Private credit took off as firms looked to fill the void caused by the retreat of banks from middle-market and other types of 'riskier' lending opportunities. PE firms offered high yields for institutional and wealthy investors, outperforming the S&P 500, the Russell 2000, and venture capital during a period of low interest rates.

Loan and Credit Risk Analysis:

Credit risk analysis extends beyond credit analysis and is the process that achieves a lender's goals by weighing the costs and benefits of taking on credit risk.

By balancing the costs and benefits of granting credit, lenders measure, analyze and manage risks their business is willing to accept.

The creditworthiness of the borrower, derived from the credit analysis process, is not the only risk lenders face. When granting credit, lenders also consider potential losses from non-performance, such as missed payments and potential bad debt. With such risks come costs, so lenders weigh them against anticipated benefits such as risk-adjusted return on capital (RAROC). Credit risk analysis determines a borrower's ability to meet their debt obligations and the lender's aim when advancing credit.

Expected losses, risk-adjusted return, and other considerations all serve to inform the outcome of the credit risk analysis process. Three factors to quantify the expected loss (cost of credit risk) include the probability of default, loss given default, and exposure at default.

Purpose of Credit Risk Analysis

Credit risk analysis aims to take on an acceptable level of risk to advance the lenders' goals. Goals can include profitability, business growth, and qualitative factors. Management crafts policies that drive their business to achieve its goals.

Although credit analysis can rate risks and estimate the probability of default, default risk is only one entity-specific risk factor. Lenders consider costs and benefits holistically when determining if the anticipated outcomes are acceptable to their business and financial exposure.

To estimate the cost of risk, lenders employ a multitude of information from the borrower, the lender, and external parties such as credit agencies. Some measures, such as credit scores and credit risk analysis models, are tools that allow lenders to estimate their expected loss (EL) via the probability of default (PD), loss-given default (LGD), and exposure at default (EAD).

The direct benefit of taking on credit risk is interest, a combination of default risk premium, liquidity premium, and other factors; however, benefits extend beyond interest revenue. For example, lenders may take on additional credit risk to grow a credit portfolio (their asset base), gain market share and expand relationships, or ensure their portfolio achieves an acceptable risk-adjusted return on capital.

Individual outcomes of credit risk analysis include granting credit with specific credit conditions or even approving exceptional credit to borrowers who may not qualify within standard policies. Management's goal is to mitigate the portfolio credit risks sufficiently to optimize the firm's accepted risks in aggregate.

For example, credit risk analysis can determine that lending in the absence of financial risk (e.g., cash-secured lending) is still not acceptable, perhaps due to headline risk specific to the borrower's owner or the industry that the company operates in.

Conversely, credit risk analysis may support lending to a newer business model (i.e., without proven cash flow) as a business strategy to expand relationships and increase exposure to a growing segment.

Credit problems and risk management

Credit risk management is a key issue that lenders of all forms must address. BIS has identified three key areas: concentration, credit processes, and market and liquidity-sensitive exposures.

Concentration reflects not the largest borrowers per se but exposures where the expected loss can sizably deplete the capital. For example, in trade credit, if a lender offers the same terms (amount, repayment, etc.) to a business with no track record and a publicly traded company, the credit concentration is considered more significant with the former compared to the latter. If this exposure has an expected loss that will deplete the lender's capital to an unacceptable level, that risk must be adjusted accordingly.

Credit processes encompass lenders' steps to assess, measure, and conduct credit risk analyses. Errors in the process lead to credit problems for the lender, for example:

- Leveraging value-at-risk (VaR) models with unvalidated tail risks and loss.
- Decisions that are not easily replicable, resulting in inconsistent results and unmanaged portfolio risk.
- Poor monitoring and control of collateral and fraud, leaving any losses higher than expected.
- Consistent mispricing and assessment of non-financial collateral in light of market conditions or business cycles, resulting in poor risk-adjusted return and higher than planned concentration risk.

Market and liquidity-sensitive exposures include foreign exchange risks, financial derivatives, and contingent liabilities. There is a difference between willingness and ability to pay, particularly for illiquid collateral or volatility, causing an outsized increase in exposure compared to the collateral value. If the borrower cannot access sufficient liquidity, the risk to the lender will rise regardless of willingness to repay. Stress testing is one way to structure and manage credit risk.

Fraud Detection and Prevention:

Banking fraud — is one of the most persistent issues financial institutions and their customers face and poses a serious threat to all parties involved. The Federal Trade Commission reports that it received 2.8 million fraud reports from consumers in 2021 alone, with total fraud losses amounting to $5.8 billion USD. Customers aren't the only ones who pay for fraud: The American Banking Journal states for every dollar lost to fraud, banks see $4 in costs — and that's without factoring in the damage fraud can do to a bank's reputation.

As banking systems have moved online, so too has fraud, with fraudsters developing their own digitized methods of stealing customers' identities and gaining access to their personal accounts. Under these conditions, it's little wonder that 96% of banking customers surveyed say that security and fraud protection is either a "somewhat" or "very" important factor when choosing a bank.

To fight fraud in digital spaces — thereby securing the loyalty of existing customers and generating new business — banks must leverage innovative technology to enhance their financial fraud detection and prevention strategies.

Common Examples of Banking Fraud

One of the most frustrating things about banking fraud is that it can take many forms, with new schemes emerging daily. After all, if there's one thing fraudsters excel at, it's pivoting. Listed below are some of the most common forms of fraud (at present) in the banking industry:

Phishing: In a phishing attack, a scammer reaches out to an individual over email, text, or even a phone call posing as their banking institution. Scammers' ultimate goal is to convince their target to click a link that loads malware, ransomware, or spyware onto their computer or to provide personally identifying information. Phishing — which is a form of social engineering — is often a gateway to other forms of banking fraud, providing criminals with a point of entry from which they can execute subsequent attacks.

Phishing is not only incredibly common, but it's also highly successful since scammers are often able to mimic legitimate institutions with alarming accuracy. What's more, phishing not only poses a threat to banking customers, but also to financial institutions themselves: Bank employees are a popular target for scammers trying to gain access to internal systems, and phishing attacks are a leading cause of corporate data breaches.

Identity theft: Perhaps the most basic form of fraud, identity theft refers to any crime that involves someone wrongfully obtaining another person's personally identifying information — such as their name, phone number, or address — and using it for fraudulent purposes. In many cases, criminals will use a banking customer's stolen identity to take ownership of that customer's online account in what is known as an account takeover attack.

Credential theft: Another basic form of fraud, credential theft involves stealing a banking customer's information. However, the scope of the attack extends beyond a customer's personally identifiable information into more confidential information, such as their ID number, password, card credentials, or Social Security number. As with identity theft, fraudsters often use these stolen credentials to stage an account takeover.

Wire fraud: Wire fraud broadly describes the use of telecommunications or the internet to defraud individuals, often across state or national borders. In the United States, wire fraud is a federal crime investigated by the Federal Bureau of Investigation. In the financial services sector, scammers trick banking customers into sending funds via wire transfer, often posing as a family member or friend in urgent need of financial assistance.

Money laundering: A form of fraud that impacts banks directly, the U.S. Department of the Treasury describes money laundering as "financial transactions in which criminals, including terrorist organizations, attempt to disguise the proceeds, sources or nature of their illicit activities."

In addition to funding illicit — and potentially dangerous — activities, money laundering compromises the integrity of the financial services marketplace and risks drawing banks into criminal networks. Any institution found party to money laundering — even unknowingly — could find itself subject not only to reputational damage and loss of goodwill but also legal and regulatory sanctions.

Application fraud: With application fraud, a scammer applies for a loan or line of credit with a bank using a stolen or synthetic identity. Once approved, the scammer will initially use the account in the expected way, making smaller purchases and scheduled repayments to create the illusion of normal account usage and gain access to new products and/or higher lines of credit. Eventually, the fraudster will make a series of large purchases with no intention of repayment before disappearing without a trace, leaving the bank on the hook for the bill. Application fraud is sometimes known as accounting fraud or account opening fraud.

While this list is a good starting point for understanding banking fraud — and fraud management in banking — it's essential to remember that fraudsters' methods are constantly evolving. To that end, here are some emerging forms of fraud to watch out for:

Fraud as a Service: A growing number of cybercriminals are offering their services up to the highest bidders in what's known as Fraud as a Service. Other offerings in the Fraud as a Service "marketplace" include fraud training tutorials for would-be threat actors and access to specialized tools and malicious software programs.

Biometrics spoofing: Although implementing biometric authentication is a smart way to enhance banking fraud protection (more on that soon enough), fraudsters have already started to find ways around these security measures. With biometrics spoofing, criminals use banking customers' photos, video clips, and even stolen fingerprints to spoof their identities for verification purposes and gain access to their accounts.

What is bank fraud and detection mechanism and Data Warehouse roles?

Bank fraud detection and prevention refers to the collective policies, protocols, procedures, and technologies financial institutions leverage to protect their assets, systems, and customers against fraud. Detection includes any activities related to threat monitoring, account monitoring, behavioral profiling, and proactive risk identification. On the prevention side, it includes any proactive measures related to threat mitigation, such as developing internal controls, conducting employee training, and implementing multi-layered security. While rule based and transactional logic can be applied in Data warehouse Technology with logic of maximum no of transactions in odd hour, unusually high transaction amount for specific customer id in different time as well as in different geography, different mobile device login with other beneficiary adds. Immediate fraud can be alarmed through automated calls as well as Outbound call centers. However, more sophisticated solution will be built using DataLake, AI, Cloud Platform

Artificial intelligence (AI) is the key to overcoming these challenges. AI-based fraud monitoring systems can ingest and parse massive quantities of data — a must, given the high volume of transactions banks process each day — and detect fraudulent activity in real-time.

Compared to rules-based engines, AI is highly adaptable, enabling banks to easily pivot their fraud management strategy based on new and emerging threats. And finally, AI offers far greater accuracy than manual or rules-based fraud detection, significantly reducing the rate of false positives and providing banking customers with a better overall experience.

Machine learning: Machine learning, a subset of AI, is a powerful tool for fraud prevention in the banking industry. Machine learning enables fraud monitoring and detection systems to "learn" from behavioral data, consortium data, and other internal and external data sources and adapt accordingly. The result is that banks are better able to navigate the increasingly complex fraud landscape and deliver more proactive protection to their customers and their assets.

Biometric authentication: Biometric authentication is an identification technique that relies on a customer's unique physical characteristics, such as their voice, facial features, or fingerprints, to verify their identity. Each of these characteristics is known as biometric data.

Biometric authentication has quickly become a popular security measure with financial institutions because customers' biometric data cannot be stolen, forgotten, or lost. Although fraudsters can spoof a customer's biometric data, it is far more challenging to do so than it is to steal their identity or credentials. To get the greatest value out of biometric authentication, banks should pair it with other technologies and controls to create a truly multi-layered security strategy.

Two-factor and/or multi-factor authentication: Two-factor (2FA) and multi-factor authentication (MFA) are identification techniques that require banking customers to provide two or more pieces of evidence to verify their identity. 2FA and MFA are fairly standard security measures that, like biometric authentication, should be layered with the other technologies shown here to create a comprehensive anti-fraud strategy.

Advanced analytics: Financial institutions process hundreds — even thousands — of transactions each day, each of which generates data. When analyzed using advanced data science techniques, customer and transaction data can be incredibly potent, enabling banks to gain a 360-degree view across the business, enhance operational efficiency, and engage in predictive fraud detection.

Regulatory Reporting:

Banks are obligated to adhere to a multitude of reporting requirements enforced by financial regulators, including BASEL, AML, KYC, and IFRS, among others. Data warehouses play a pivotal role in streamlining this compliance process by centralizing the requisite data and facilitating the generation of precise and timely reports for submission. These regulatory bodies, spanning the globe and including entities such as the Bank for International Settlements (BIS), Financial Stability Board (FSB), OCC (USA), Federal Reserve System (USA), Financial Conduct Authority (FCA, UK), ECB, BOJ, MAS, RBI, and others, mandate numerous reports to uphold the integrity of financial systems, preserve legal compliance, foster confidence in the banking sector, and safeguard the interests of consumers and investors

Alarming Facts for Regulatory Non-Compliance in Banking $243 billion has been fined on bank because of noncompliance since 2008. $937.7 Million Dollar has been charged because of AML and KYC noncompliance and Data Privacy regulation.

Current Outlook: Why Does it Need Attention?

Many regulatory reporting processes are internal to the organization, but there is a regulatory body that oversees compliance. These regulatory bodies are dependent on the industry that the organization is part of. For the BFSI vertical, it is the Fellow Chartered Accountant (FCA), the energy industry is Office of Gas and Electricity Markets (Ofgem), advertising is ITC and the communications industry is "The Office of Communications" (Ofcom).

Like most regulatory bodies, FCA and others engage in periodic reviews. During these checks, they not only check what your organization is doing at that moment but also a back story to that point. Some of the most common forms of regulatory reporting in practice today include:

Complaint Handling Process: The complaint handling process checks how the business handles complaints and the official procedures in place to make sure it is productive and fair. Once the business has established a fair and process-driven system, the business should adhere to it and also make sure it conforms to regulation.

Training: This has to do with the processes the business puts in place for performance reviews, appraisals, CPD, and on-the-job training. Regulatory reporting ensures all of these processes are fair and above board to the parties involved.

Procedures and Processes: These check all the processes and procedures for operation in an organization regardless of how complex or diverse they may be. These processes are as intricate as the method of signing paperwork, explaining terms and conditions to customers, and others like that. All of these are examples of regulatory reporting as it is mandated and regulated.

Record Keeping: This is the basic form of regulatory reporting that most organizations do in some form or the other. It is the process of keeping and maintaining accurate, detailed, and accessible records of all the transactions carried out as regulatory bodies check it. These records also include the organization's adherence to process in whatever form that may take. It should also cover penalties for whenever anyone deviates from the specified protocol.

Challenges Banks and Other Financial Organizations Face with Regulatory Reporting

Banks find it difficult to keep up with the fast-changing and increasing regulatory requirements. The fast pace, increased complexity, and granularity in the regulatory reporting requirements are putting banks under more pressure even with stretched budgets and resources. This challenge is more apparent for banks that cut across several regulatory jurisdictions and many of these organizations are constantly looking for ways to standardize reporting and stretch data models.

Data integrity and quality

with less than effective data quality frameworks. Studies show that 31% of institutions view data quality as a major challenge to effectively meet all the compliance requirements. Also, analysts spend a lot of their time in data collection and organization duties making them spend less time on data analysis.

Legacy Systems and processes

Core systems are dependent on many manual processes and multiple independent systems to meet up several complex requirements. It puts immense pressure on time, accuracy, resourcing, and efficiency. This inflexibility affects adaptability to the constantly evolving regulatory requirements.

Emerging Trends in Regulatory Reporting

Technology is at the center of developing a culture of a comprehensive and proactive approach to help regulatory reporting. Compliance has gone beyond adding new resources for better effectiveness as it has shown that a gradual and planned adoption of new gen technologies such as AI, Cloud and Big data technologies etc, can help handle the challenge banks and other financial institutions are facing. While most banks have implemented regulatory reporting in the Data Warehouse in an effective way. But considerable volume and reduced time span from regulator time to time forcing banks to do the regulatory reporting in AI, Cloud and Bigdata.

Customer Churn Prediction:

Customer churn is a common problem across businesses in many sectors. If you want to grow as a company, you have to invest in acquiring new clients. Every time a client leaves, it represents a significant investment lost. Both time and effort need to be channeled into replacing them. Being able to predict when a client is likely to leave, and offer them incentives to stay, can offer huge savings to a business.

As a result, understanding what keeps customers engaged is extremely valuable knowledge, as it can help you to develop your retention strategies, and to roll out operational practices aimed at keeping customers from walking out the door.

Predicting churn is a fact of life for any subscription business, and even slight fluctuations in churn can have a significant impact on your bottom line. We need to know: "Is this customer going to leave us within X months?" Yes or No? It is a binary classification task.

What are the main challenges in Customer Churn Implementation?

Churn prediction modeling techniques attempt to understand the precise customer behaviors and attributes that signal the risk and timing of customers leaving. It's not a walk-in-the-park task so I will mention just four points to consider.

To succeed at retaining customers who are ready to abandon your business, Marketers & Customer Success experts must be able to predict in advance which customers are going to churn and set up a plan of marketing actions that will have the greatest retention impact on each customer. The key here is to be proactive and engage with these customers. While simple in theory, the realities involved with achieving this "proactive retention" goal are extremely challenging.

The accuracy of the technique is critical to the success of any proactive retention efforts. If the Marketer is unaware of a customer about to churn, no action will be taken to retain that customer.

Special retention-focused offers or incentives may be provided to happy, active customers, resulting in reduced revenues for no good reason.

Your churn prediction model should rely on (almost) real-time data to quantify the risk of churning, not on static data. Although you will be able to identify a certain percentage of at-risk customers with even static data, your predictions will be inaccurate.

Cross-Selling and Upselling:

It's well known that the cost of selling to existing customers is far cheaper than the cost of acquiring new ones. In fact, it can cost five times more to attract a new customer.

That's why effective cross-selling — the process of offering current customers complementary products or services — is so beneficial in banking. So much so that it has remained a key focus of financial institutions' business strategy over the past several years.

But it's getting more difficult. Changes heightened by today's digital age have decreased cross-selling opportunities; bankers have less face-to-face interaction with customers and increasingly disparate product lines. And as customers demand more personalization in their banking experiences, traditional cross-sell techniques are becoming less effective.

Digital technologies can give financial institutions the insight they need to better serve their customers and significantly boost their cross-selling effectiveness. Technology solutions help financial institutions use existing customer information such as recent purchases, important life events, and future goals to make more personalized, beneficial, and relevant offers.

Let's take a look at a hypothetical scenario for a first-time home buyer, Sandra:

Sandra applies for a mortgage online and receives a message during her application suggesting that she opens a checking account at the same time, so that it is easier to make payments.

The information garnered during the application tells the bank that Sandra is a first-time homebuyer and therefore might be looking for a line of credit to purchase high-value new items for her house, such as furniture and kitchen appliances.

A personalized email is then sent to her, offering a special rate on a credit card based on her custom creditworthiness score. The email includes a link to an application, which is pre-filled with the information Sandra has already provided when she took out the mortgage, so she can complete the remaining fields in a matter of minutes.

This level of personalization is what makes a digital cross-selling process more successful. Rather than feeling bombarded with irrelevant offers, customers are more receptive to this approach. In fact, 70% of digital customers said they would be highly interested in receiving tailored insurance offers from their banks based on their transaction data. What's more, customers are more than twice as interested in these offers if they have recently experienced a significant life event or made a major purchase.

Utilizing data from a data warehouse, banks can identify opportunities for cross-selling and upselling to existing customers. By understanding their financial needs and behavior, banks can offer relevant products and services, increasing customer engagement and loyalty.

1.4 Architecture for Banking Data Warehouse:

Source System Analysis:

Determine the origins of the necessary data within the bank. These sources may encompass core banking systems, transactional databases, CRM systems, payment processing systems, LOS (Loan Origination System), LMS (Loan Management System), digital systems, channels such as IB/MB, WhatsApp, digital lending journeys, document systems, as well as a range of core systems in wholesale banking such as FX trading, credit risk, market risk, liquidity risk, TMS (Treasury Management System), and DMS (Document Management System), among others

1.5 Source System Integration with DWH:

It is important to understand a few concepts like ETL vs. ELT the Loading part of the Source Data in EDW.

Extract, Transform, Load (ETL) first extracts the data from a pool of data sources, which are typically transactional databases. The data is held in a temporary staging database. Transformation operations are then performed, to structure and convert the data into a suitable form for the target data warehouse system. The structured data is then loaded into the warehouse, ready for analysis.

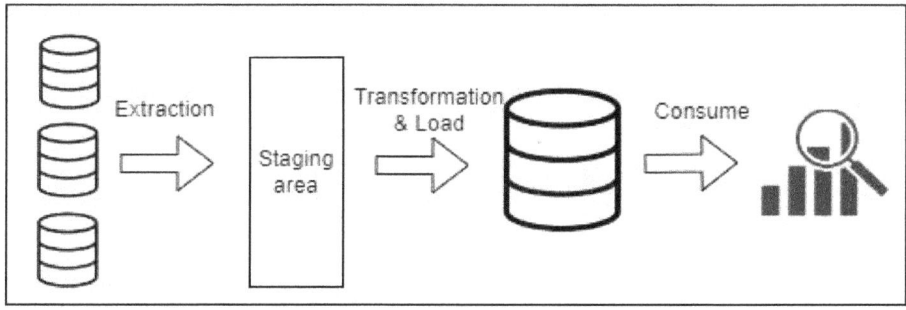

Fig 1.11: ETL Process

With Extract Load Transform (ELT), data is immediately loaded after being extracted from the source data pools. There is no staging database, meaning the data is immediately loaded into the single, centralized repository. The data is transformed inside the data warehouse system for use with business intelligence tools and analytics.

Fig 1.12: ELT Process

Extract, Transform, Load (ETL) Process in Bank:

The ETL (Extract, Transform, Load) process is a foundational approach for integrating data into a Data Warehouse (DWH). This process entails extracting data from various banking source systems, transforming it to align with the DWH's schema and data model, and subsequently loading it into the DWH. Many banks commonly utilize ETL tools such as Informatica and DataStage for this purpose.

The process typically involves running batch jobs at the end of each day (EOD). These jobs extract data based on control files or control tables from the source systems, temporarily storing it in a staging server designated for the DWH. Informatica Power Center jobs then operate on this staging data to populate Dimension and Fact Tables. In most cases, this data refresh occurs within the T-1 Day timeframe.

Additionally, many Mart jobs, often constructed using Power Center, are executed once the Dimension is created, either through DB Link or Informatica ETL processes. These jobs contribute to the final population of the Data Mart, which serves as the Operational Data Store (ODS). Subsequently, data may flow downstream to destinations like Branch Analytics and Risk Mart.

The Data Warehouse platform itself may be built using specialized appliances such as Teradata or Netezza, or a combination of Oracle Exadata systems coupled with Informatica Power Center. The architectural framework is depicted below.

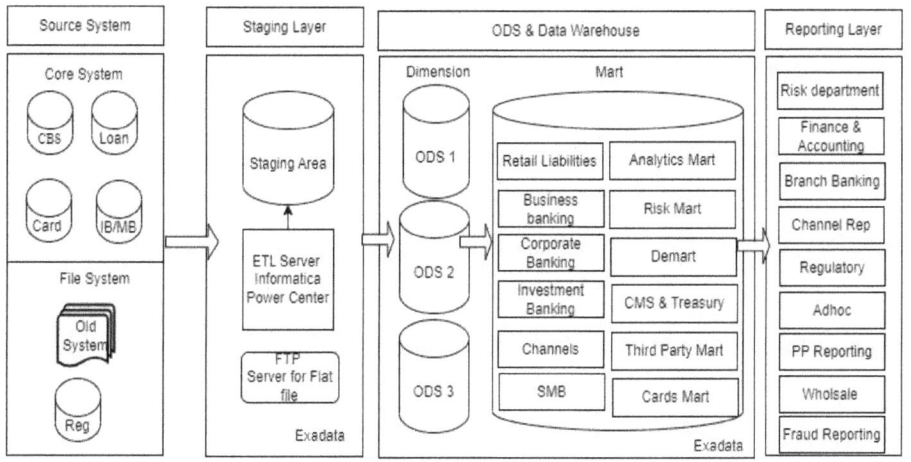

Fig 1.13: EDW Architecture

Data Replication:

In some cases, banks use data replication techniques to continuously replicate data from source systems to the DWH. This ensures that the DWH is always up-to-date with the latest data. This refers to Flash copy of the Source system data, Where DBA takes the Flash copy of Source System data post EOD and loads into the MIS/Reporting System. This is useful particularly when there is old records/History data has to be maintained and Reports based on history is required. This technique refers to Export/Import using many DB Utilities.

1.6 Change Data Capture (CDC):

Change Data Capture (CDC) is a technique employed to identify and capture only the alterations made to source data since the previous data integration process. This approach significantly reduces data processing overhead and expedites the data integration procedure. CDC facilitates real-time data transmission from source to destination using mechanisms like Redo log, Archive Logs. Commonly used platforms for CDC include GG (Golden Gate), IBM CDC, and Attunity.

Most CDC platforms operate in a similar fashion, with a few offering the convenience of a web-based user interface for configuring source, target, and schema details. CDC also manages DDL changes dynamically to accommodate Schema Drift, permitting the application of filters on columns to be ingested.

CDC offers the capability to replicate historical data once and subsequently transmits deltas in real time. These CDC tools boast a broad range of adopters, linking various database source systems like Oracle, DB2, Postgres, MySQL, Netezza, Teradata, MS SQL, and more to targets including RDBMS and NoSQL databases like Big Data and Cloud storage solutions such as AWS S3, RDS, DynamoDB, Azure ADLS Gen3, Synapse, Cosmos, GCP Cloud Storage, and BigQuery. I am giving example of GG as one of CDC tool and detailing of various Process and design behind it to do the Job

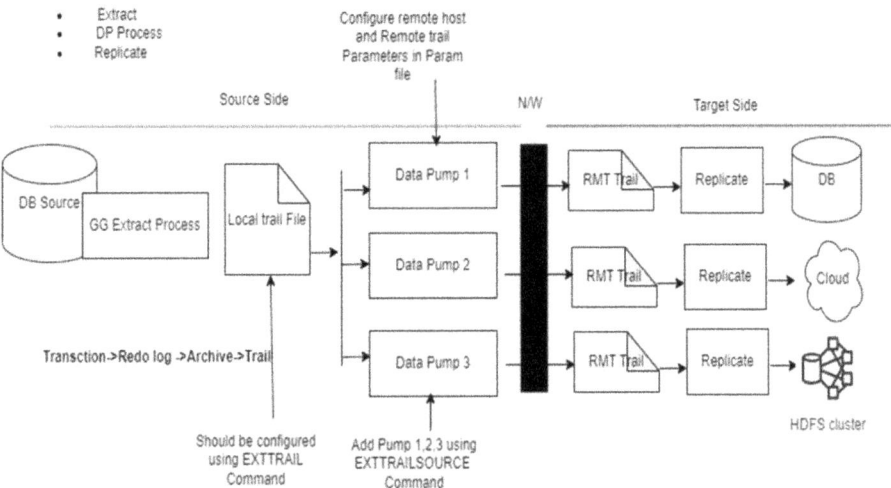

Fig 1.14: CDC Golden Gate Data Extraction Mechanism

The following process elucidates how Golden Gate (GG) operates within an Oracle database for the sake of comprehension. The Golden Gate process comprises three components: Extract, Pump, and Replicate

Redo Log Extraction:

Oracle databases maintain a record of all changes made to the database in redo logs. The redo log files capture the before and after images of the data for each transaction, enabling recovery and replication processes. Oracle Golden Gate uses the LogMiner utility within the Oracle database to read and extract data from the redo log files. Log Miner analyzes the redo log files and converts the captured data changes into a format that can be consumed by Oracle Golden Gate.

Oracle Golden Gate generates "trail files" that contain the captured data changes from the redo logs. Tail files are temporary storage files that hold the transactional data changes until they are ready to be transmitted to the target system or data warehouse.

Oracle Golden Gate can perform data transformation as needed. Data transformation includes data filtering, data mapping, and data format conversion to ensure that the data is aligned with the business requirement.

Pump Process:

The Pump process is responsible for reading the trail files generated by the Extract process and transporting them to the target system(s). Depending on the deployment and configuration, the Pump process can be activated on the source system, the target system, or a dedicated separate system. Different architectures are employed for this platform, such as Classic and Integrated deployments.

In the Classic Deployment, the Golden Gate agent operates within the Data Center of the source system and generates trail files there. However, this is an older approach and can occasionally burden the source system, potentially causing performance issues.

On the other hand, the Integrated Deployment involves a separate system designated to store all the redo log and trail files. This approach minimizes the impact on the source system and is the industry's current preferred method. Nevertheless, it may necessitate the careful setup of additional servers and infrastructure.

The Pump process plays a crucial role in ensuring that data changes are delivered in the sequence they occurred, preserving the integrity and consistency of the data throughout the replication process.

Replicate Process:

The Replicate process is activated on the target system to apply the data changes received from the Pump process to the target database.

the Replicate process reads the trail files received from the Pump process. It processes the data changes in the same order they were captured in the trail files. It ensures that data changes are applied in the correct sequence and transactions are committed in the target database to maintain data consistency.

The Replicate process communicates with the Pump process to acknowledge the receipt and successful application of data changes. Checkpoints are used to track the progress of data replication and ensure data consistency between the source and target systems.

In the event of replication failures, the Replicate process incorporates robust error-handling and recovery mechanisms to guarantee data integrity and the resumption of replication. For SQL-driven systems as the target, there is an SQL adapter designed to connect with databases like Oracle, MSSQL, MySQL, DB2, and others. In parallel, a NoSQL adapter is available to establish connections with NoSQL databases such as those on AWS, GCP, Azure, Cloudera Hadoop Systems, Documentdb, Cassandra, and Neo4J.

1.7 API Integration:

In certain scenarios, API integration stands out as the preferred choice, often favored by architects. This approach is particularly advantageous for tasks such as retrieving available balances, returning response codes, and enabling the IB/MB App to connect with the core system for a wide array of banking operations.

In the realm of modern application systems built upon a Microservices Architecture, the inclination is to exchange data via APIs rather than relying on database integration. API integration is particularly effective when connecting with the DataMart Serving Layer, facilitating real-time or on-demand data retrieval with high throughput. Technologists typically leverage an ESB Layer and API gateway to circumvent peer-to-peer integration challenges, providing enterprise-level services. IBM's MQ Platform also offers various API integration options, complete with security control mechanisms within the ESB Layer.

While the API Layer primarily operates using a Synchronization Mechanism, it also offers asynchronous options when required.

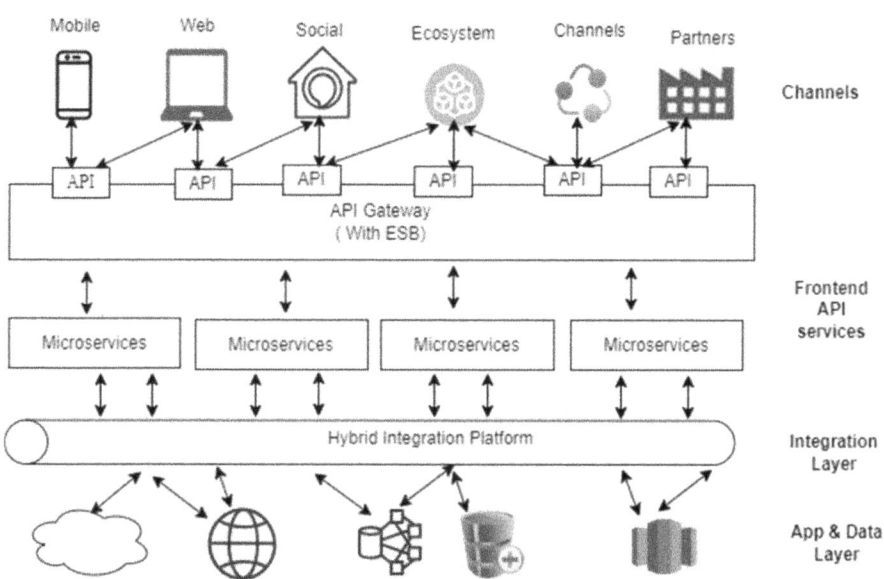

Fig 1.15: API integration with various ecosystems

API Documentation & Credentials:

Creating great API documentation is a delicate balancing act between providing detailed technical information and displaying it in a way that is easy to consume. The best way to see how it should be done is to look at examples of businesses that are doing well – thankfully, they're not hard to find.

Many popular tools publish their API documentation online so that 3rd-party developers can get easy access to them. Stripe and Twilio are two great examples of documentation done right. Although their solutions are developed in-house, the best practice they display is still useful for businesses looking to create their own API documentation. Here are a few of the reasons why these sets of documentation are so effective:

They provide example code in the documentation so that users can see how it works in practice. They make it easy to find solutions to common problems so that busy developers can get what they need quickly.

They don't provide unnecessary information that isn't required to understand the API and how it works. When users are busy working and hit a problem, they want usable documentation, not extraneous information. They don't assume a certain level of knowledge – the simplest concepts are as fully-explained as the most difficult ones. They are well-formatted. The content is organized and consistent and easy to read. This reduces friction for users who are looking to learn or solve a problem.

Understand the API you want to integrate by reading its documentation. The documentation provides information about the endpoints, parameters, request methods, authentication methods, response formats, and usage guidelines. Many APIs require authentication, often through API keys or access tokens. You may need to sign up for an account with the API provider to obtain these credentials.

Choose Integration Method:

APIs can be integrated using various methods, such as REST (Representational State Transfer), SOAP (Simple Object Access Protocol), GraphQL, or other custom protocols. Choose the appropriate method based on the API's capabilities and your project requirements.

Develop Integration Code:

Write code in your application to send requests to the API endpoints and handle the responses. This code will typically be in the programming language you are using for your application. Implement proper error handling in your integration code to deal with situations where the API may not respond or return errors. Testing and deployment of the integrated code to your production environment, ensuring that it continues to work correctly in the Live system. Few API specification industries follow, however, Open API is widely used

OpenAPI (formerly Swagger) – The most popular specification. Open-source, and backed by companies such as Microsoft and Google. Uses JSON objects with a specific schema to describe API elements.

RAML – YAML-based, RAML (or RESTful API Modeling Language) takes a top-down approach to create documentation that is clear, consistent, and precise.

API Blueprint – Another open-source specification, API Blueprint is designed to be highly accessible. It uses a description language that is similar to Markdown and excels in situations where a design-first philosophy is followed during API creation.

Below are various Integration Tooling and Popular Platforms :

Postman:

Postman is a widely-used API testing and development tool that allows you to send API requests, inspect responses, and test various API endpoints easily.

Swagger/OpenAPI:

Swagger is a set of open-source tools that helps you design, build, document, and consume RESTful APIs. It provides a standard for describing APIs using the OpenAPI Specification. Similarly Integromat, Zapier are popular automation tools that connect different apps and services.

Cloud API Platform:

Apigee is an API management platform that helps you design, secure, deploy, monitor, and scale APIs. If you're using Amazon Web Services (AWS), the AWS API Gateway allows you to create, deploy, and manage APIs at scale. If you're using Google Cloud Platform (GCP), Google Cloud Endpoints enables you to deploy, manage, and monitor APIs on GCP.

Direct Database Connection:

Banks can establish direct connections to the source system databases, allowing them to query and extract data directly for integration into the DWH. In this approach, many of database connections are through DBLink and JDBC/ODBC Connections. However, In banking world, this connection is established to the DR or Reporting system so that it won't generate any back pressure to the source system while users run the query. Sometimes, the DWH system integrates with Materialized View to avoid DB Pressure with direct access.

Chapter 2: Data Virtualization:

Data virtualization is a core technology where the DWH retrieves and integrates data on-demand from source systems without physically moving or replicating the data. Establishes a single data-access layer for finding and using all enterprise data, consisting of logical/virtual representations of physical data sources like data warehouses, data lakes, transactional and analytical databases, cloud and enterprise applications' data services and APIs, and data files. With this centralized, logical layer, data virtualization enables real-time access to data stored across multiple heterogeneous data sources.

Logical data management, powered by data virtualization, reduces data integration and delivery costs while boosting management efficiency and agility. This provides an important role in enabling our business users to garner valuable information through self- service reporting.

This provides real-time access to data without creating redundant copies. Various platforms used for this are like IBM Data Virtualization, Denode etc.

Below, we'll illustrate how Virtualization operates and explore its various use cases. These use cases encompass Data Fabric, Hybrid and Multi-Cloud Data Integration, Self-Service Business Intelligence for diverse branch banking operations, Data Governance, Enterprise Data Services, and Data Mesh.

When complex queries are initiated from the front-end system, they are directed to the Virtualization Layer, as exemplified by Denodo in this context. Denodo receives these queries, generates an execution plan, employs its Query Optimization technology along with AI/ML recommendations, comprehends how different source systems should be interconnected, and constructs an efficient plan for data retrieval to deliver to the requester. Throughout this execution, it manages aspects such as data governance, security, and cataloging. Additionally, it presents data in views with a universal semantic model, facilitating delivery to various BI, Data Science tools, and APIs, among others.

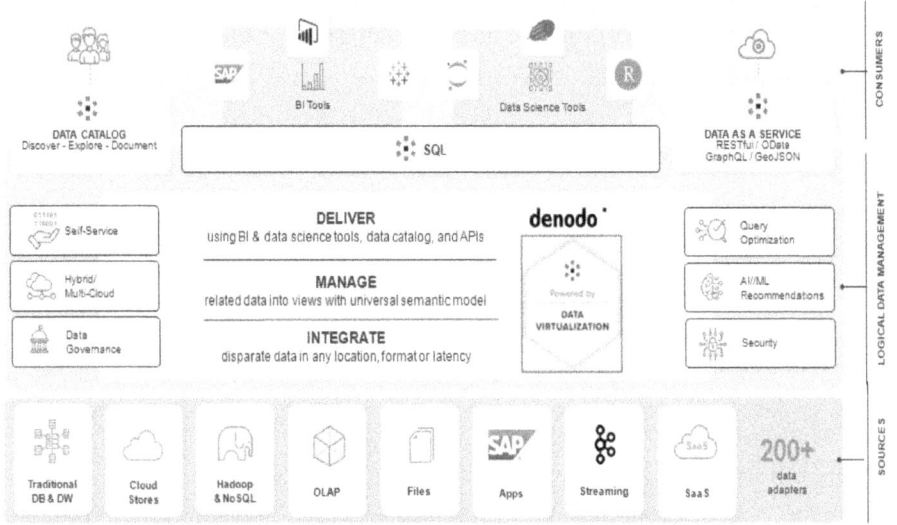

Fig 2.1 – Data Visualization Platform

Data Quality and Cleansing: Before integrating data into the DWH, data quality checks and cleansing procedures are performed to ensure the accuracy, consistency, and completeness of the data along with various index/Partition for performance purpose

Data Encryption and Security: Data encryption and security measures are implemented during the data integration process to protect sensitive banking data during transmission and storage. Various Mechanisms are being used for the same. PCI/DSS for Cards data and other PII/SPDI Data, RSA 256/1024/2048 is being used along with Security keys And tokens for retrieval process.

Chapter 3: Metadata Management:

Metadata about the integrated data, including data definitions, data lineage, and data relationships, is documented and managed to provide context and meaning to the data in the DWH.

Metadata includes information about the various data elements stored in the data warehouse, such as their names, descriptions, data types, lengths, and formats. This helps users and administrators understand the meaning and characteristics of each data element.

Data lineage metadata tracks the origin, transformation, and movement of data throughout the data warehouse. It shows how data is sourced, transformed, and loaded from different systems, providing a clear picture of data transformations and dependencies.

Metadata includes access permissions, roles, and security-related information for different datasets and tables within the data warehouse. This helps ensure data security and compliance with privacy regulations.

Metadata encompasses information pertaining to indexes, partitions, and other performance-related configurations, all of which play a crucial role in enhancing query performance within the data warehouse.

Numerous catalog platform providers offer solutions for managing metadata. These include well-known names like Microsoft Purview, Alation Data Catalog, Collibra Data Intelligence Cloud, Informatica Cloud Data Governance Catalog, Oracle EME, SAP PowerDesigner, Alex, IBM Watson Catalog, Data Brick Unity Catalog, and more.

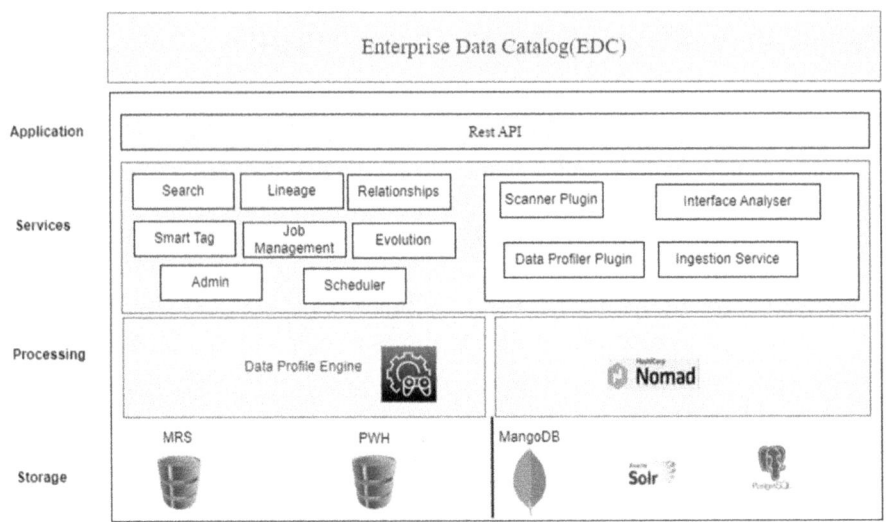

Fig 3.1: Informatica Enterprise Data Catalog Architecture

3.1 Summary of First Generation

Data warehousing has become indispensable for organizations aiming to harness their data for competitive advantages. By providing a centralized, well-structured, and accessible data repository, data warehouses empower businesses to uncover insights that drive innovation, streamline operations, and fuel growth. In the ever-evolving landscape of technology, data warehousing remains a foundational component of contemporary data management strategies. It is poised to continue shaping the arena of data-driven decision-making for years to come.

In this context, we explore various mechanisms for data ingestion, including database and file-based approaches, leading to staging data. We delve into the population of Dimension and Fact tables, followed by data mart consumption by the reporting layer. To ensure data quality and synchronization across job runs, we implement an ABC Framework (Audit, Balance, and CheckSum) alongside a control table. Complex job dependencies are managed through schedulers like AutoSys, Control-M, which are equipped with dependency checks and directed acyclic graph (DAG) processes.

Furthermore, the ecosystem includes automated alerts for job failures, monitoring, and multi-level support (L1, L2, L3) as essential components to maintain business as usual (BAU) operations. Security Information and Event Management (SIEM) systems and observability platforms are employed to monitor infrastructure health and facilitate necessary repairs. Recently, solutions like AppDynamics and Dynatrace have emerged as suitable SIEM platforms, offering graphical health checks for systems, including job monitoring.

CDO Functions encompass Data Quality, Metadata Management, and Business Glossary development. The Catalog operates in harmony with the Enterprise Data Warehouse (EDW) to enhance data governance and empower project teams with swift data discovery capabilities. Data Warehouses are ideally suited for handling structured and well-understood data types. The majority of organizations rely on Data Warehouse platforms for various purposes, including MIS, regulatory reporting, product development, and self-service analytics.

We explored several banking use cases that can be effectively addressed through the use of Data Warehouses. We delved into various conceptual models that are essential components of the Warehouse and hold significant importance. It's noteworthy that even today, a substantial portion of regulatory and compliance projects relies on Data Warehouses as their foundation. Additionally, we discussed a range of integration mechanisms, including databases, Change Data Capture (CDC), APIs, Enterprise Service Bus (ESB), and other technical layers, which are pivotal for maintaining control and ensuring Information Security Governance (ISG) during data transfer across databases, microservices, and applications.

PART 2: Second Generation

Chapter 4: Bigdata Platform

Social media platforms generate a substantial volume of data, much of which is machine-generated. This data emanates from various sources, including sensor data, RFID tags, handheld devices, and meters. Of all these sources, social networks have emerged as a prominent and pertinent component of Big Data discussions today.

To illustrate the scale, consider Twitter, which produces an astounding 12 terabytes of tweet data every single day in the year 2011. It's worth noting that these figures are challenging to pinpoint precisely due to their constantly changing nature. The key takeaway here is the sheer magnitude of these numbers. Regardless of whether these statistics become outdated in a couple of years, they remain so enormous that they cannot be effectively managed using traditional approaches alone.

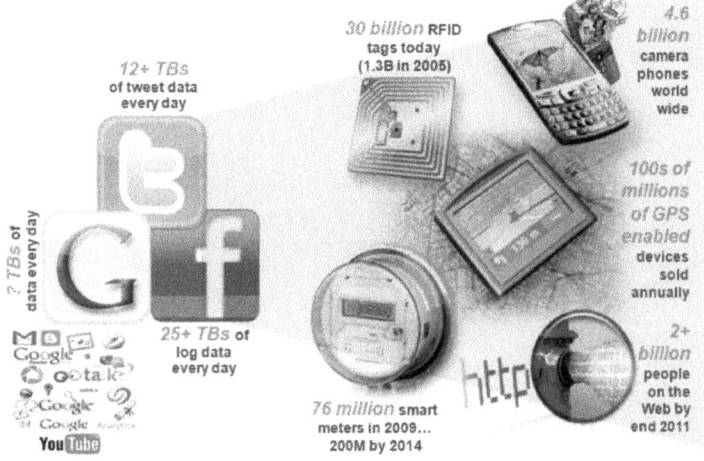

Fig 4.1: Sources of Data in 2011

In the year 2010, Facebook was generating a staggering 25 terabytes of log data daily, with an estimated 7 to 8 terabytes of data being shared on the Internet. When it comes to Google, it's a vast landscape encompassing Google Plus, YouTube, Google Maps, and numerous other services, making it challenging to quantify. This constitutes the left-hand side of our data landscape—the social network layer.

Now, let's return to the realm of data instrumentation. The contemporary technological landscape offers an array of tools and technologies that facilitate unprecedented interconnectivity. This interconnectivity isn't limited to just person-to-person (P2P) interactions; it extends to machine-to-machine (M2M) connections as well. Once again, the precise numbers may fluctuate, but the key takeaway is the sheer magnitude of these figures, which continues to defy our imagination.

With over 4.6 billion camera phones equipped with built-in GPS for tagging photo locations, purpose-built GPS devices, and the widespread use of smart meters, the world is teeming with data sources. Consider the example of the bridge in Minneapolis, USA, that collapsed several years ago. It was reconstructed with embedded smart sensors capable of measuring concrete contraction and flex in response to weather conditions, ice accumulation, and more.

Reflecting on Sam P's launch of Smart Planet, I initially perceived it as a marketing ploy. However, the reality is that our world has become profoundly instrumented, interconnected, and intelligent. This transformation enables us to tackle novel challenges and gain insights that were previously unimaginable. This is the essence of the Big Data opportunity. Below, we outline the scope that has propelled the rise of Big Data. This data is often too large and complex to be processed and analyzed using traditional data processing methods. Big data is characterized by the three Vs: Variety, Volume, Velocity

Variety -Today, our data analytics capabilities have evolved to encompass a diverse range of data types. In the past, technological limitations constrained our ability to efficiently and cost-effectively analyze data. However, this landscape has transformed dramatically. We now have the capacity to analyze not only vast quantities of non-relational data but also various formats, including video, audio, and text, opening up countless possibilities. Big data comes in different formats and types, such as structured data (e.g., databases), semi-structured data (e.g., XML, JSON), and unstructured data (e.g., text, images, videos). Analyzing this diverse data requires specialized technologies and tools

Volume -Furthermore, there's a compelling case for analyzing and managing all available data, rather than relying on subsets. Imagine the enhanced accuracy and depth of insight achievable by leveraging years of data to build models instead of relying on just a few months' worth. It comes from various sources, including social media, sensors, transactions, logs, and more.

Velocity: The data is generated and collected at high speeds in real-time or near real-time. This requires efficient processing and analysis to derive valuable insights promptly.

Low latency - analytics is another critical aspect. Many data types, especially newer ones, have a remarkably short lifespan. If you fail to take immediate action upon receiving this data, it becomes essentially useless.

IM Systems-One recurring use case involves augmenting existing Information Management (IM) systems. Many retail customers, for instance, maintain extensive historical data in their Teradata warehouses. However, they typically access only a fraction of this data, often for specialized analytics rather than standard sales reports. Extracting older data becomes a cumbersome process, requiring SQL programming and off-hours execution, while the cost of storing this underutilized data continues to mount."

Analyze Information in Motion
- Smart Grid Management
- Multi Model Simulation
- Real time Promotions
- CyberSecurity
- ICU Monitoring
- Options Trading
- Click stream analysis
- CDR Processing
- IT Log analysis
- RFID Tracking & Analysis

Analyze Variety of information
- Social media/Sentimental Analysis
- Geospatial Analysis
- Brand Strategy
- Scientific Research
- Epidemic Early warning sysetm
- Market Analysis
- Video Analysis
- Audio Analysis

Analyze Extreme Volume of Information
- Transctional Analysis to create insight
- Fraud Modelling and detection
- Risk Modelling & Management
- Social Media/Senitmental Anaysis
- Environment Analysis
- Operational Analytics -BI Reporting
- Planning and forcasting Analysis
- Predictive Analysis

Discovery & Experimentation
- Brand Strategy
- Scientific Research
- Banking and finance
- Model Developement
- Hypothesis Testing
- Ad hoc Analysis

Fig 4.2: Various use case for Big Data during inception

4.1 What is Hadoop?

Traditional applications work on the model where data is loaded into memory from wherever it is stored onto the computer where the application is run. As Google was processing ever increasing amounts of internet data, the IT people there quickly realized that this centralized approach to computation was not sustainable. So, they decided to move to a model where they would scale out their processing and storage and created a system where the data would be processed on the machine where it is stored. This processing technology became MapReduce and the storage model is known as the Google File System (GFS), which is a direct descendant to today's HDFS.

Hadoop is a top-level Apache project being built and used by a global community of contributors. Yahoo has been the largest contributor to the project, and it uses Hadoop extensively across its businesses. One of its employees, Doug Cutting, reviewed key papers from Google and concluded that the technologies they described could solve the scalability problems of Nutch, an open-source Web search technology. So, Cutting led an effort to develop Hadoop (which, incidentally, he named after his son's stuffed elephant).

Hadoop is particularly well-suited to batch-oriented, read-intensive applications. Key features include the ability to distribute and manage data across a large number of nodes and disks. By using the Map Reduce programming model with the Hadoop framework, programmers can create applications that automatically take advantage of parallel processing. A single commodity box consisting of, let's say, a single CPU and disk, forms a node in Hadoop. Such boxes can be combined into clusters, and new nodes can be added to a cluster without an administrator or programming changing the format of the data, how the data was loaded, or how the jobs (programming logic) were written.

The following overview of Hadoop was extracted from the Hadoop wiki at http://wiki.apache.org/hadoop/

Apache Hadoop is a framework for running applications on large clusters built of commodity hardware. The Hadoop framework transparently provides applications with both reliability and data motion.

Hadoop Explained two key concepts: Map Reduce

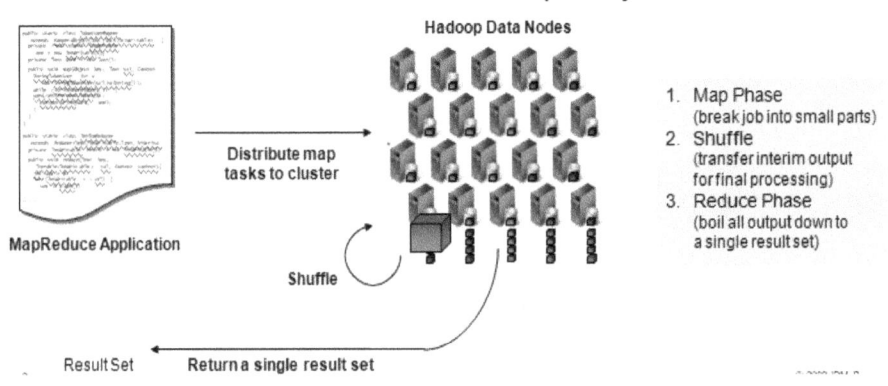

Fig 4.3: Map Reduce Explained

Hadoop implements a computational paradigm named Map/Reduce, where the application is divided into many small fragments of work, each of which may be executed or re-executed on any node in the cluster. In addition, it provides a distributed file system (HDFS) that stores data on the compute nodes, providing very high aggregate bandwidth across the cluster. Both Map/Reduce and the distributed file system are designed so that node failures are automatically handled by the framework.

Map Reduce is a software framework introduced by Google to support distributed computing on large data sets of clusters of computers. The Hadoop Distributed File System (HDFS) is where Hadoop stores its data. This file system spans all the nodes in a cluster. Effectively, HDFS links together the data that resides on many local nodes, making the data part of one big file system.

Furthermore, HDFS assumes nodes will fail, so it replicates a given chunk of data across multiple nodes to achieve reliability. The degree of replication can be customized by the Hadoop administrator or programmer. However, by default is to replicate every chunk of data across 3 nodes: 2 on the same rack, and 1 on a different rack.

4.1.1 Map Reduce Basic:

The only feasible approach to tackling large-data problems today is to divide and conquer, a fundamental concept in computer science that is introduced very early in typical undergraduate curricula. The basic idea is to partition a large problem into smaller subproblems. They can be tackled in parallel by different workers—threads in a processor core, cores in a multi-core processor, multiple processors in a machine, or many machines in a cluster. Intermediate results from each individual worker are then combined to yield the final output. I am writing more details of the Map Reduce framework in this paragraph.

For example, the following are just some of the issues that need to be addressed:

• How do we break up a large problem into smaller tasks? More specifically, how do we decompose the problem so that the smaller tasks can be executed in parallel?

• How do we assign tasks to workers distributed across a potentially large number of machines (while keeping in mind that some workers are better suited to running some tasks than others, e.g., due to available resources, locality constraints, etc.)?

• How do we ensure that the workers get the data they need?

• How do we coordinate synchronization among the different workers?

• How do we share partial results from one worker that is needed by another?

• How do we accomplish all of the above in the face of software errors and hardware faults?

Algorithm of MAP Reduce framework:

Key-value pairs form the basic data structure in MapReduce is basic principle. Keys and values may be primitives such as integers, floating point values, strings, and raw bytes, or they may be arbitrarily complex structures (lists, tuples, associative arrays, etc.). Programmers typically need to define their own custom data types. In MapReduce, the programmer defines a mapper and a reducer with the following signatures:

map: $(k1, v1) \rightarrow [(k2, v2)]$

reduce: $(k2, [v2]) \rightarrow [(k3, v3)]$

Below Pseudo Concept for basic Mapper /Reducer

class Mapper method Map(docid a, doc d) for all term t doc d do Emit(term t, count 1)	class Reducer method Reduce(term t, counts [c1, c2, . . .]) sum ← 0 ,for all count c counts [c1, c2, . . .] do, sum ← sum + c Emit(term t, count sum)

Input key-values pairs take the form of (docid, doc) pairs stored on the distributed file system, where the former is a unique identifier for the document, and the latter is the text of the document itself. The mapper takes an input key-value pair, tokenizes the document, and emits an intermediate key-value pair for every word: the word itself serves as the key, and the integer one serves as the value (denoting that we've seen the word once). The MapReduce execution framework guarantees that all values associated with the same key are brought together in the reducer. Therefore, in our word count algorithm, we simply need to sum up all counts (ones) associated with each word. The reducer does exactly this, and emits final key value pairs with the word as the key, and the count as the value. Final output is written to the distributed file system, one file per reducer. Words within each file will be sorted by alphabetical order, and each file will contain roughly the same number of words.

4.1.2 Partitioners and combiner in the MapReduce Framework:

There are two additional elements that complete the programming model: partitioners and combiners. Partitioners are responsible for dividing up the intermediate key space and assigning intermediate key-value pairs to reducers. In other words, the partitioner specifies the task to which an intermediate key-value pair must be copied. Within each reducer, keys are processed in sorted order (which is how the "group by" is implemented). The PARTITIONERS AND COMBINERS simplest partitioner involves computing the hash value of the key and then taking the mod of that value with the number of reducers. This assigns approximately the same number of keys to each reducer (dependent on the quality of the hash function). Note, however, that the partitioner only considers the key and ignores the value—therefore, a roughly-even partitioning of the key space may nevertheless yield large differences in the number of key-value pairs sent to each reducer (since different keys may have different numbers of associated values). This imbalance in the amount of data associated with each key is relatively common in many text processing applications due to the Zipfian distribution of word occurrences.

Combiners are an optimization in MapReduce that allow for local aggregation before the shuffle and sort phase. We can motivate the need for combiners by considering the word count algorithm, which emits a key-value pair for each word in the collection. Furthermore, all these key-value pairs need to be copied across the network, and so the amount of intermediate data will be larger than the input collection itself. This is clearly inefficient. One solution is to perform local aggregation on the output of each mapper, i.e., to compute a local count for a word over all the documents processed by the mapper. With this modification (assuming the maximum amount of local aggregation possible), the number of intermediate key-value pairs will be at most the number of unique words in the collection times the number of mappers (and typically far smaller because each mapper may not encounter every word). The combiner in MapReduce supports such an optimization. One can think of combiners as "mini-reducers" that take place on the output of the mappers, prior to the shuffle and sort phase. Each combiner operates in isolation and therefore does not have access to intermediate output from other mappers. The combiner is provided with keys and values associated with each key (the same types as the mapper output keys and values). Critically, one cannot assume that a combiner will have the opportunity to process all values associated with the same key. The combiner can emit any number of key-value pairs, but the keys and values must be of the same type as the mapper output (same as the reducer input).12 In cases where an operation is both associative and commutative (e.g., addition or multiplication), reducers can directly serve as combiners. In general, however, reducers and combiners are not interchangeable

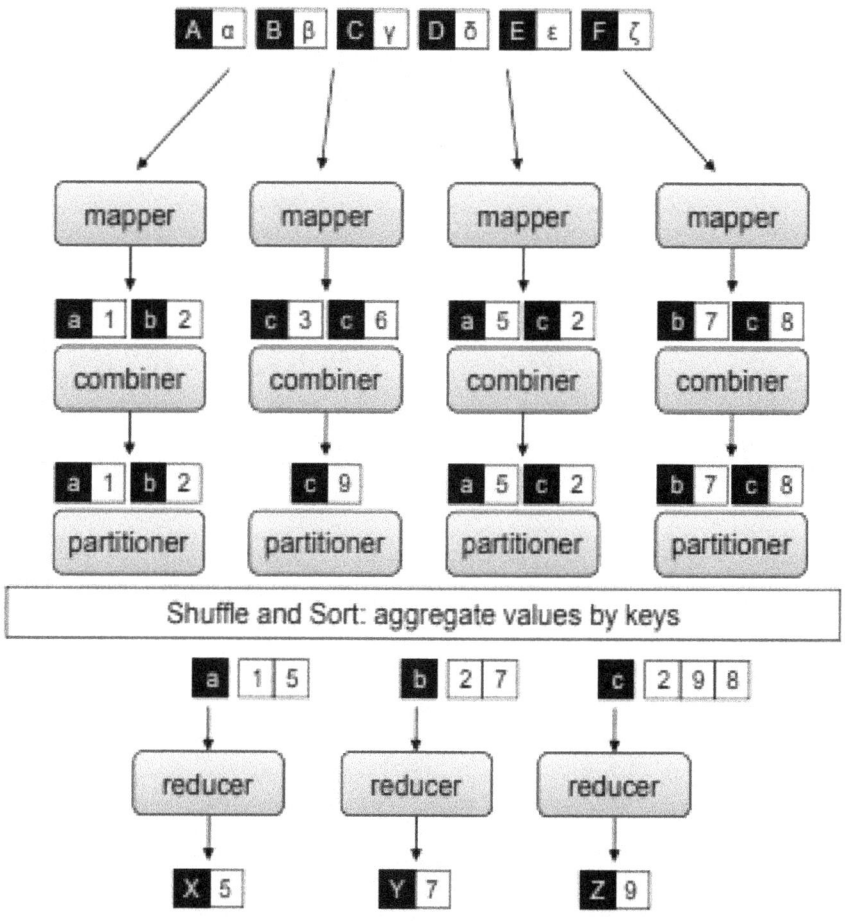

Fig 4.4: Complete view of MapReduce, illustrating combiners and partitioners in addition to Mappers and reducers. Combiners can be viewed as "mini-reducers" in the map phase. Partitioners determine which reducer is responsible for a particular key.

4.1.3 Distributed File System:

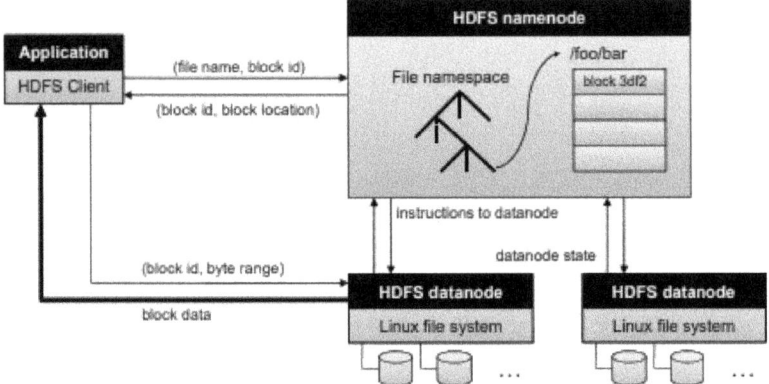

Fig 4.5: The Architecture of HDFS

The namenode (master) is responsible for maintaining the file namespace and directing clients to datanodes (slaves) that actually hold data blocks containing user data

In HDFS, an application client wishing to read a file (or a portion thereof) must first contact the namenode to determine where the actual data is stored. In response to the client request, the namenode returns the relevant block id and the location where the block is held (i.e., which datanode). The client then contacts the datanode to retrieve the data. Blocks are themselves stored on standard single-machine file systems, so HDFS lies on top of the standard OS stack (e.g., Linux). An important feature of the design is that data is never moved through the namenode. Instead, all data transfer occurs directly between clients and datanodes; communications with the namenode only involve transfer of metadata. By default, HDFS stores three separate copies of each data block to ensure both reliability, availability, and performance. In large clusters, the three replicas are spread across different physical racks, so HDFS is resilient towards two common failure scenarios: individual datanode crashes and failures in networking equipment that bring an entire rack offline. Replicating blocks across physical machines also increases opportunities to co-locate data and processing in the scheduling of MapReduce jobs, since multiple copies yield more opportunities to exploit locality.

The namenode is in periodic communication with the datanodes to ensure proper replication of all the blocks: if there aren't enough replicas (e.g., due to disk or machine failures or to connectivity losses due to networking equipment failures), the namenode directs the creation of additional copies;16 if there are too many replicas (e.g., a repaired node rejoins the cluster), extra copies are discarded. To create a new file and write data to HDFS, the application client first contacts the namenode, which updates the file namespace after checking permissions and making sure the file doesn't already exist. The namenode allocates a new block on a suitable datanode, and the application is directed to stream data directly to it. From the initial datanode, data is further propagated to additional replicas. In the most recent release of Hadoop as of this writing (release 0.20.2), files are immutable—they cannot be modified after creation. There are current plans to officially support file appends in the near future, which is a feature already present in GFS.

In summary, the HDFS namenode has the following responsibilities:

• Namespace management. The namenode is responsible for maintaining the file namespace, which includes metadata, directory structure, file to block mapping, location of blocks, and access permissions. These data are held in memory for fast access and all mutations are persistently logged.

• Coordinating file operations. The namenode directs application clients to datanodes for read operations, and allocates blocks on suitable datanodes for write operations. All data transfers occur directly between clients and datanodes. When a file is deleted, HDFS does not immediately reclaim the available physical storage; rather, blocks are lazily garbage collected.

• Maintaining overall health of the file system. The namenode is in periodic contact with the datanodes via heartbeat messages to ensure the integrity of the system. If the namenode observes that a data block is under-replicated (fewer copies are stored on datanodes than the desired replication factor), it will direct the creation of new replicas. Finally, the namenode is also responsible for rebalancing the file system.17 During the course of normal operations, certain data nodes may end up holding more blocks than others; rebalancing involves moving blocks from datanodes with more blocks to datanodes with fewer blocks. This leads to better load balancing and more even disk utilization.

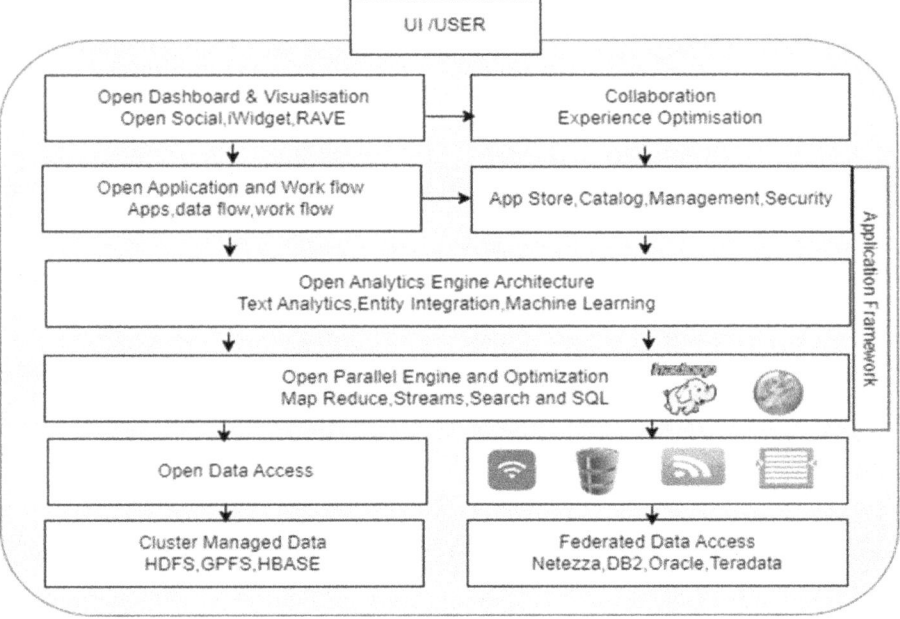

Fig 4.6: Year 2010 - Initial Hadoop Framework and Functional Architecture

4.2 Hbase –NO SQL Framework:

It didn't take long for all these new ideas to begin condensing into open-source implementations. In the years following, the data management space has come to host all manner of projects. Some focus on fast key-value stores, whereas others provide native data structures or document-based abstractions. Equally diverse are the intended access patterns and data volumes these technologies support. Some forgo writing data to disk, sacrificing immediate persistence for performance. Most of these technologies don't hold ACID guarantees as sacred. Although proprietary products do exist, the vast majority of the technologies are open- source projects. Thus, these technologies as a collection have come to be known as NoSQL. Where does HBase fit in? HBase does qualify as a NoSQL store. It provides a key value API, although with a twist not common in other key-value stores. It promises strong consistency so clients can see data immediately after it's written. HBase runs on multiple nodes in a cluster instead of on a single machine. It doesn't expose this detail to its clients. Your application code doesn't know if it's talking to 1 node or 100, which makes things simpler for everyone. HBase is designed for terabytes to petabytes of data, so it optimizes for this use case. It's a part of the Hadoop ecosystem and depends on some key features, such as data redundancy and batch processing, to be provided by other parts of Hadoop. Below are the few of demand where Hbase has come into picture in early days.

4.2.1 Hbase and Bigtable – Solution for Web search Problem:

Searching is the process of finding specific information that matters to you. For instance, it could involve looking up relevant sections in a textbook or finding web pages containing the information you need. When you search for documents containing specific terms, it involves referring to indexes that link terms to the documents where they appear. To make searching possible, you must construct these indexes. This is precisely what search engines like Google do. Their document database comprises the entire internet, and the search terms are the words or phrases you enter in the search box. Bigtable, and by extension, HBase, serves as the storage solution for this vast collection of documents. Bigtable offers the capability to access individual rows, allowing web crawlers to insert and update documents one at a time. The search index can be efficiently generated through MapReduce directly against Bigtable, and individual document results can be retrieved with ease. These capabilities were pivotal in shaping the design of Bigtable.

Interestingly, a technology initially designed to store a constantly updated version of the internet has proven to be quite versatile in other internet-related applications. HBase has found valuable roles within and around social networking companies. It has become a crucial part of the infrastructure for entities like Facebook, Twitter, and StumbleUpon, where it is utilized for storing communications between users and conducting communication analytics."

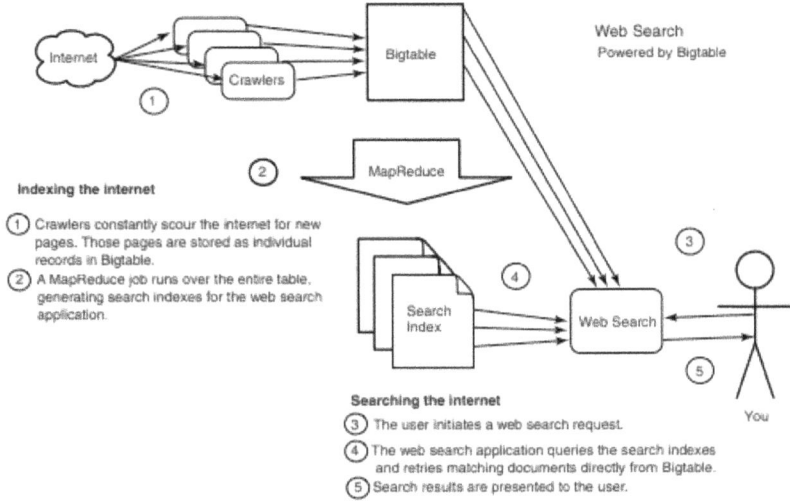

Fig 4.7: Web Search Crawler using Hbase

Capturing User interaction Data:

Monitoring encompasses one category of captured metrics. Another important category involves metrics related to user interactions with a product. How does one keep tabs on the activities of millions of site visitors? How can we determine which site features are the most popular? How do we leverage one page view to influence the next, such as tracking who viewed what and how often a specific button was clicked? Consider the example of the Like button on Facebook and the Stumble and +1 buttons on StumbleUpon. These buttons essentially count user interactions, presenting a counting challenge. Each time a user likes a particular topic, a counter increment. While StumbleUpon initially relied on MySQL, the growing popularity of the service outpaced the capabilities of MySQL clusters. In response, StumbleUpon transitioned to HBase. Although HBase lacked some essential features at the time, StumbleUpon took the initiative to implement atomic increment in HBase and contributed this enhancement back to the project.

Similarly, Facebook utilizes counters in HBase to tally the number of times users like specific pages. Content creators and page owners receive near real-time metrics regarding their page likes, enabling them to make more informed content-generation decisions. Facebook developed a system called Facebook Insights, which necessitated a scalable storage solution. The company evaluated various options, including RDBMS, in-memory counters, and Cassandra, before selecting HBase. This choice allows Facebook to scale horizontally and serve millions of users while leveraging its expertise in managing large-scale HBase clusters. The system manages tens of billions of events daily and records hundreds of metrics.

Advertisement Impressions and Click Stream:

Online advertisements have become a major source of revenue for web-based products. The model has been to provide free services to users but have ads linked to them that are targeted to the user using the service at the time. This kind of targeting requires detailed capturing and analysis of user-interaction data to understand the user's profile. The ad to be displayed is then selected based on that profile. Fine-grained user-interaction data can lead to building better models, which in turn leads to better ad targeting and hence more revenue. But this kind of data has two properties: it comes in the form of a continuous stream, and it can be easily partitioned based on the user. In an ideal world, this data should be available to use as soon as it's generated, so the user-profile models can be improved continuously without delay—that is, in an online fashion.

Content Serving:

One of the major use cases of databases traditionally has been that of serving content to users. Applications that are geared toward serving different types of content are backed by databases of all shapes, sizes, and colors. These applications have evolved over the years, and so have the databases they're built on top of. A vast amount of content of varied kinds is available that users want to consume and interact with. In addition, accessibility to such applications has grown, owing to this burgeoning thing called the internet and an even more rapidly growing set of devices that can connect to it. The various kinds of devices lead to another requirement: different devices need the same content in different formats. That's all about users consuming content

The bottom line is that users consume and generate a lot of content. HBase is being used to back applications that allow a large number of users interacting with them to either consume or generate content. When looking for ways to expand its database arsenal to include distributed database systems, Salesforce evaluated the full spectrum of NoSQL technologies before deciding to implement HBase.12 The primary factor in the choice was consistency. Bigtable-style systems are the only architectural approach that combines seamless horizontal scalability with strong record-level consistency. Additionally, Salesforce already used Hadoop for doing large offline batch processing, so the company was able to take advantage of in-house expertise in running and administering systems on the Hadoop stack.

4.3 Apache Spark – Engine replaced Hadoop Map Reduce Framework:

The Hadoop ecosystem included both a storage system (the Hadoop file system, designed for low-cost storage over clusters of commodity servers) and a computing system (MapReduce), which were closely integrated together. However, this choice makes it difficult to run one of the systems without the other. More important, this choice also makes it a challenge to write applications that access data stored anywhere else. Although Spark runs well on Hadoop storage, today it is also used broadly in environments for which the Hadoop architecture does not make sense, such as the public cloud (where storage can be purchased separately from computing) or streaming applications.

Apache Spark—a unified computing engine and set of libraries for big data—into its key components: Unified Spark's key driving goal is to offer a unified platform for writing big data applications. What do we mean by unified? Spark is designed to support a wide range of data analytics tasks, ranging from simple data loading and SQL queries to machine learning and streaming computation, over the same computing engine and with a consistent set of APIs. The main insight behind this goal is that real-world data analytics tasks—whether they are interactive analytics in a tool such as a Jupyter notebook, or traditional software development for production applications—tend to combine many different processing types and libraries.

Spark's focus on defining a unified platform is the same idea behind unified platforms in other areas of software. For example, data scientists benefit from a unified set of libraries (e.g., Python or R) when doing modeling, and web developers benefit from unified frameworks such as Node.js or Django.

Computing engine at the same time that Spark strives for unification, it carefully limits its scope to a computing engine. By this, we mean that Spark handles loading data from storage systems and performing computation on it, not permanent storage as the end itself. You can use Spark with a wide variety of persistent storage systems, including cloud storage systems such as Azure Storage and Amazon S3, distributed file systems such as Apache Hadoop, key-value stores such as Apache Cassandra, and message buses such as Apache Kafka. However, Spark neither stores data long term itself, nor favors one over another. The key motivation here is that most data already reside in a mix of storage systems. Data is expensive to move so Spark focuses on performing computations over the data, no matter where it resides. In user facing APIs, Spark works hard to make these storage systems look largely similar so that applications do not need to worry about where their data is.

Libraries Spark's final component is its libraries, which build on its design as a unified engine to provide a unified API for common data analysis tasks. Spark supports both standard libraries that ship with the engine as well as a wide array of external libraries published as third-party packages by the open-source communities. Today, Spark's standard libraries are actually the bulk of the open- source project: the Spark core engine itself has changed little since it was first released, but the libraries have grown to provide more and more types of functionalities. Spark includes libraries for SQL and structured data (Spark SQL), machine learning (MLlib), stream processing (Spark Streaming and the newer Structured Streaming), and graph analytics (GraphX). Beyond these libraries, there are hundreds of open- source external libraries ranging from connectors for various storage systems to machine learning algorithms.

Origins and Inception:

Apache Spark began at UC Berkeley in 2009 as the Spark research project, which was first published the following year in a paper entitled "Spark: Cluster Computing with Working Sets" by Matei Zaharia, Mosharaf Chowdhury, Michael Franklin, Scott Shenker, and Ion Stoica of the UC Berkeley AMPlab. At the time, Hadoop MapReduce was the dominant parallel programming engine for clusters, being the first open-source system to tackle data-parallel processing on clusters of thousands of nodes. The AMPlab had worked with multiple early MapReduce users to understand the benefits and drawbacks of this new programming model, and was therefore able to synthesize a list of problems across several use cases and begin designing more general computing platforms. In addition, Zaharia had also worked with

Hadoop users at UC Berkeley to understand their needs for the platform—specifically, teams that were doing large-scale machine learning using iterative algorithms that needed to make multiple passes over the data.

4.3.1 Spark's basic Architecture:

Typically, when you think of a "computer," you think about one machine sitting on your desk at home or at work. This machine works perfectly well for watching movies or working with spreadsheet software. However, as many users likely experience at some point, there are some things that your computer is not powerful enough to perform. One particularly challenging area is data processing. Single machines do not have enough power and resources to perform computations on huge amounts of information (or the user probably does not have the time to wait for the computation to finish). A cluster, or group, of computers, pools the resources of many machines together, giving us the ability to use all the cumulative resources as if they were a single computer. Now, a group of machines alone is not powerful, you need a framework to coordinate work across them. Spark does just that, managing and coordinating the execution of tasks on data across a cluster of computers. The cluster of machines that Spark will use to execute tasks is managed by a cluster manager like Spark's standalone cluster manager, YARN, or Mesos. We then submit Spark Applications to these cluster managers, which will grant resources to our application so that we can complete our work

Spark Applications:

Spark Applications consist of a driver process and a set of executor processes. The driver process runs your main() function, sits on a node in the cluster, and is responsible for three things: maintaining information about the Spark Application; responding to a user's program or input; and analyzing, distributing, and scheduling work across the executors (discussed momentarily). The driver process is absolutely essential—it's the heart of a Spark Application and maintains all relevant information during the lifetime of the application. The executors are responsible for actually carrying out the work that the driver assigns them. This means that each executor is responsible for only two things: executing code assigned to it by the driver, and reporting the state of the computation on that executor back to the driver node. Figure 2-1 demonstrates how the cluster manager controls physical machines and allocates resources to Spark Applications. This can be one of three core cluster managers: Spark's standalone cluster manager, YARN, or Mesos. This means that there can be multiple Spark Applications running on a cluster at the same time.

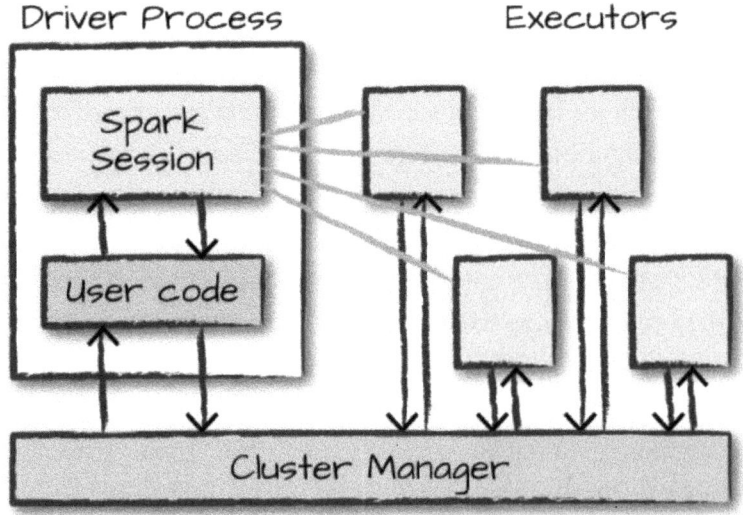

Fig 4.8: The Architecture of Spark Application

In this Fig 3.1 we can see the driver on the left and four executors on the right. In this diagram, we removed the concept of cluster nodes. The user can specify how many executors should fall on each node through configurations.

Here are the key points to understand about Spark Applications at this point:

Spark employs a cluster manager that keeps track of the resources available. The driver process is responsible for executing the driver program's commands across the executors to complete a given task. The executors, for the most part, will always be running Spark code. However, the driver can be "driven" from a number of different languages through Spark's language APIs.

Spark's language APIs make it possible for you to run Spark code using various programming languages. For the most part, Spark presents some core "concepts" in every language; these concepts are then translated into Spark code that runs on the cluster of machines. If you use just the Structured APIs, you can expect all languages to have similar performance characteristics. Here's a brief rundown: Scala Spark is primarily written in Scala, making it Spark's "default" language. Spark has two commonly used R libraries: one as a part of Spark core (SparkR) and another as an R community-driven package (sparklyr).

Fig 4.9: The relationship between the Spark Session and Spark's Language API

The SparkSession:

As discussed in the beginning of this chapter, you control your Spark Application through a driver process called the SparkSession. The SparkSession instance is the way Spark executes user-defined manipulations across the cluster. There is a one-to-one correspondence between a SparkSession and a Spark Application. In Scala and Python, the variable is available as spark when you start the console. Let's go ahead and look at the SparkSession in both Scala and/or Python

In Scala, you should see something like the following:

res0: org.apache.spark.sql.SparkSession = org.apache.spark.sql.SparkSession@...

DataFrames:

A DataFrame is the most common Structured API and simply represents a table of data with rows and columns. The list that defines the columns and the types within those columns is called the schema. You can think of a DataFrame as a spreadsheet with named columns.

Figure 2-3 illustrates the fundamental difference: a spreadsheet sits on one computer in one specific location, whereas a Spark DataFrame can span thousands of computers. The reason for putting the data on more than one computer should be intuitive: either the data is too large to fit on one machine or it would simply take too long to perform that computation on one machine.

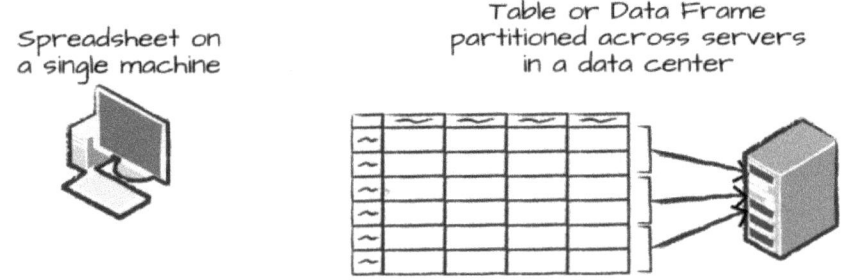

Fig 4.10: Distributed vs Single Machine Analysis

Partitions:

To allow every executor to perform work in parallel, Spark breaks up the data into chunks called partitions. A partition is a collection of rows that sit on one physical machine in your cluster. A DataFrame's partitions represent how the data is physically distributed across the cluster of machines during execution. If you have one partition, Spark will have a parallelism of only one, even if you have thousands of executors. If you have many partitions but only one executor, Spark will still have a parallelism of only one because there is only one computation resource. An important thing to note is that with DataFrames you do not (for the most part) manipulate partitions manually or individually. You simply specify high-level transformations of data in the physical partitions, and Spark determines how this work will actually execute on the cluster. Lower-level APIs do exist (via the RDD interface),

Transformations:

In Spark, the core data structures are immutable, meaning they cannot be changed after they're created. This might seem like a strange concept at first: if you cannot change it, how are you supposed to use it? To "change" a DataFrame, you need to instruct Spark how you would like to modify it to do what you want. These instructions are called transformations. Let's perform a simple transformation to find all even numbers in our current DataFrame:

// in Scala val divisBy2 = myRange.where("number % 2 = 0")

Notice that these return no output. This is because we specified only an abstract transformation, and Spark will not act on transformations until we call an action (we discuss this shortly). Transformations are the core of how you express your business logic using Spark. There are two types of transformations: those that specify narrow dependencies, and those that specify wide dependencies. Transformations consisting of narrow dependencies (we'll call them narrow transformations) are those for which each input partition will contribute to only one output partition. In the preceding code snippet, the where statement specifies a narrow dependency, where only one partition contributes to at most one output partition,

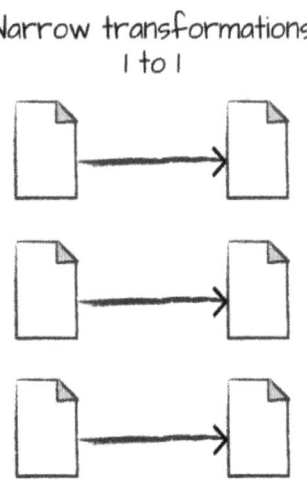

Fig 4.11: A Narrow dependency

A wide dependency (or wide transformation) style transformation will have input partitions contributing to many output partitions. You will often hear this referred to as a shuffle whereby Spark will exchange partitions across the cluster. With narrow transformations, Spark will automatically perform an operation called pipelining, meaning that if we specify multiple filters on DataFrames, they'll all be performed in-memory. The same cannot be said for shuffles. When we perform a shuffle, Spark writes the results to disk.

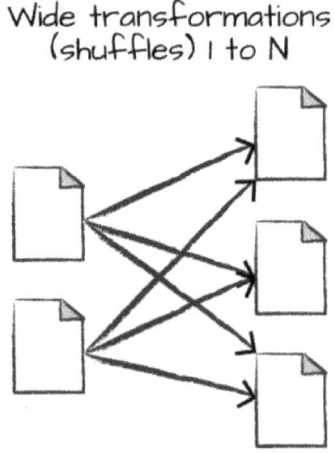

Fig 4.12: A wide dependency

You'll see a lot of discussion about shuffle optimization across the web because it's an important topic, but for now, all you need to understand is that there are two kinds of transformations. You now can see how transformations are simply ways of specifying different series of data manipulation. This leads us to a topic called lazy evaluation.

Lazy Evaluation:

Lazy evaluation means that Spark will wait until the very last moment to execute the graph of computation instructions. In Spark, instead of modifying the data immediately when you express some operation, you build up a plan of transformations that you would like to apply to your source data. By waiting until the last minute to execute the code, Spark compiles this plan from your raw DataFrame transformations to a streamlined physical plan that will run as efficiently as possible across the cluster. This provides immense benefits because Spark can optimize the entire data flow from end to end. An example of this is something called predicate pushdown on DataFrames. If we build a large Spark job but specify a filter at the end that only requires us to fetch one row from our source data, the most efficient way to execute this is to access the single record that we need. Spark will actually optimize this for us by pushing the filter down automatically.

Actions:

Transformations allow us to build up our logical transformation plan. To trigger the computation, we run an action. An action instructs Spark to compute a result from a series of transformations. The simplest action is count, which gives us the total number of records in the DataFrame:

Div is By2.count()

The output of the preceding code should be 500. Of course, count is not the only action. There are three kinds of actions: Actions to view data in the console Actions to collect data to native objects in the respective language Actions to write to output data sources In specifying this action, we started a Spark job that runs our filter transformation (a narrow transformation), then an aggregation (a wide transformation) that performs the counts on a per partition basis, and then a collect, which brings our result to a native object in the respective language. You can see all of this by inspecting the Spark UI, a tool included in Spark with which you can monitor the Spark jobs running on a cluster.

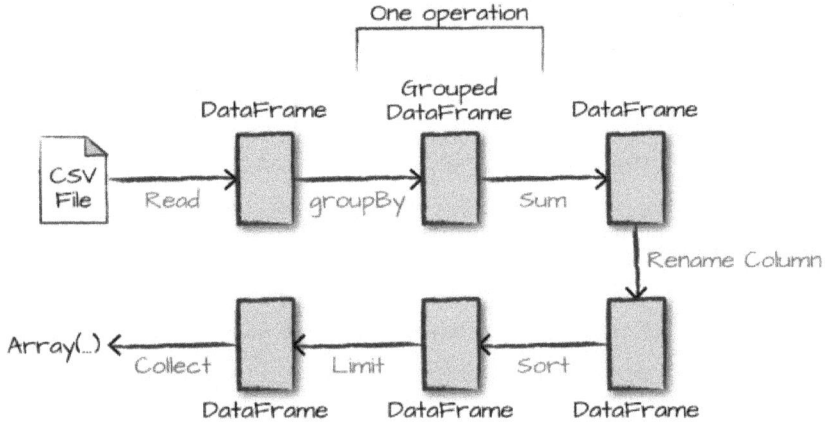

Fig 4.13: The entire DataFrame transformation flow

The first step is to read in the data. We defined the DataFrame previously but, as a reminder, Spark does not actually read it in until an action is called on that DataFrame or one derived from the original DataFrame.

The second step is our grouping; technically when we call groupBy, we end up with a Relational Grouped Dataset, which is a fancy name for a DataFrame that has a grouping specified but needs the user to specify an aggregation before it can be queried further. We basically specified that we're going to be grouping by a key (or set of keys) and that now we're going to perform an aggregation over each one of those keys.

Therefore, the third step is to specify the aggregation. Let's use the sum aggregation method. This takes as input a column expression or, simply, a column name. The result of the sum method call is a new DataFrame. You'll see that it has a new schema but that it does know the type of each column. It's important to reinforce (again!) that no computation has been performed. This is simply another transformation that we've expressed, and Spark is simply able to trace our type information through it.

The fourth step is a simple renaming. We use the with Column Renamed method that takes two arguments, the original column name and the new column name. Of course, this doesn't perform computation: this is just another transformation!

The fifth step sorts the data such that if we were to take results off of the top of the DataFrame, they would have the largest values in the destination total column. You likely noticed that we had to import a function to do this, the desc function. You might also have noticed that desc does not return a string but a Column. In general, many DataFrame methods will accept strings (as column names) or Column types or expressions. Columns and expressions are actually the exact same thing. Penultimately, we'll specify a limit. This just specifies that we only want to return the first five values in our final DataFrame instead of all the data. The last step is action!

Spark has several core abstractions: Datasets, DataFrames, SQL Tables, and Resilient Distributed Datasets (RDDs). These different abstractions all represent distributed collections of data. The easiest and most efficient are DataFrames, which are available in all languages

Resilient Distributed Datasets (RDD): RDD is Spark's fundamental data structure, which represents an immutable distributed collection of objects. RDDs can be processed in parallel across a cluster, providing fault tolerance and data lineage. RDDs were one of the key innovations that made Spark stand out from other big data processing frameworks at the time.

Spark Core and Expanding APIs: Initially, Spark's core API was primarily built around the RDD abstraction. However, over time, Spark expanded its APIs to include DataFrames and Datasets, which provided more structured and optimized processing capabilities, making it easier for users to work with structured and semi-structured data.

Spark Streaming: Spark Streaming was introduced to provide real-time stream processing capabilities. It leverages a micro-batch processing model, where data is processed in small batches, enabling low-latency and near-real-time analytics on data streams.

MLlib: MLlib is Spark's machine learning library, designed to simplify the development of scalable machine learning algorithms. It provides a wide range of algorithms and utilities for tasks such as classification, regression, clustering, and collaborative filtering.

Spark SQL: Spark SQL offers integration with structured data, allowing users to run SQL queries directly on Spark data. This integration facilitates seamless data processing and querying using SQL, data frames, and datasets, making it easier for data analysts and SQL users to work with Spark.

Structured Streaming: Building upon Spark Streaming, Structured Streaming was introduced to provide a high-level, declarative API for stream processing. It enables users to express their streaming computations as a series of batch-like operations on continuous data streams. Project Tungsten was a major initiative within the Spark project to improve the performance and memory efficiency of Spark. It involved a complete redesign of Spark's execution engine and memory management, resulting in significant performance gains.

Spark on Kubernetes: While Spark initially relied on Hadoop YARN for cluster resource management, it evolved to run natively on Kubernetes as well. Kubernetes offers more flexibility and streamlined resource management, making it easier to deploy and manage Spark clusters. Spark continued to integrate with other big data technologies and ecosystems, such as Apache HBase, Apache Hive, and Apache Kafka, further expanding its capabilities and use cases.

4.3.2 Delta Lake:

Delta Lake is an open-source storage layer that provides ACID (Atomicity, Consistency, Isolation, Durability) transactions on top of Spark. It enables data versioning, schema evolution, and reliability, making data management more robust in Spark environments. The Spark ecosystem continued to grow with numerous third-party libraries and extensions, addressing various use cases like graph processing (GraphX), data streaming (Spark Streaming and Structured Streaming), and data integration (Spark connectors for various data sources).

While the majority of use cases we have discussed so far pertain to batch processing and computation of structured/unstructured data, we also have a growing need for real-time applications that demand a scalable Publish-Subscribe (Pub Sub) messaging platform.

Chapter 5:
Demand of Real time and Streaming:

While the main focus of this real time and streaming topic is the building of event-driven systems of different sizes, there is a deeper focus on software that spans many teams. This is the realm of service-oriented architectures- an idea that arose around the start of the century, where a company reconfigures itself around shared services that do commonly useful things.

This idea became quite popular. Amazon famously banned all intersystem communications by anything that wasn't a service interface. Later, upstart Netflix went all in on micro services, and many other web-based startups followed suit. Enterprise companies did similar things, but often using messaging systems, which have a subtly different dynamic. Much was learned during this time, and there was significant progress made, but it wasn't straightforward.

One lesson learned, which was pretty ubiquitous at the time, was that service based approaches significantly increased the probability of you getting paged at 3 a.m., when one or more services go down. In hindsight, this shouldn't have been surprising. If you take a set of largely independent applications and turn them into a web of highly connected ones, it doesn't take too much effort to imagine that one important but flaky service can have far-reaching implications, and in the worst case bring the whole system to a halt. As Steve Yegge put it in his famous Amazon/Google post, "Organizing into services taught teams not to trust each other in most of the same ways they're not supposed to trust external developers."

What did work well for Amazon, though, was the element of organizational change that came from being wholeheartedly service based. Service teams think of their software as being a cog in a far larger machine. As Ian Robinson put it, "Be of the web, not behind the web." This was a huge shift from the way people-built applications previously, where intersystem communication was something, teams reluctantly bolted on as an afterthought. But the services model made 3 interactions a first-class entity. Suddenly your users weren't just customers or businesspeople; they were other applications, and they really cared that your service was reliable. So, applications became platforms, and building platforms is hard.

LinkedIn felt this pain as it evolved away from its original, monolithic Java application into 800–1,100 services. Complex dependencies led to instability, versioning issues caused painful lockstep releases, and early on, it wasn't clear that the new architecture was actually an improvement

A good example is the regulation that hit the finance industry in January 2018, which states that trading activity has to be reported to a regulator within one minute of it happening. A minute may seem like a long time in computing terms, but it takes only one batch-driven system, on the critical path in one business silo, for that to be unattainable. So, the banks that had gone to the effort of installing real-time trade eventing, and plumbed it across all their product-aligned silos, made short work of these regulations. For the majority that hadn't it was a significant effort, typically resulting in half-hearted, hacky solutions.

So, enterprise companies start out complex and disconnected- many separate, asynchronous islands—often with users of their own—operating independently of one another for the most part. Internet companies are different, starting life as simple, front-facing web applications where users click buttons and expect things to happen. Most start as monoliths and stay that way for some time (arguably for longer than they should). But as internet companies grow and their business gets more complex, they see a similar shift to asynchronicity. New teams and departments are introduced and they need to operate independently, freed from the synchronous bonds that tie the frontend.

So ubiquitous desires for online utilities, like making a payment or updating a shopping basket

But messaging is no panacea. Enterprise service buses (ESBs), for example, have vocal detractors and traditional messaging systems have a number of issues of their own. They are often used to move data around an organization, but the absence of any notion of history limits their value. So, even though recent events typically have more value than old ones, business operations still need historical data—whether it's users wanting to query their account history, some service needing a list of customers, or analytics that need to be run for a management report. On the other hand, data services with HTTP-fronted interfaces make lookups simple. Anyone can reach in and run a query. But they don't make it so easy to move data around. To extract a dataset, you end up running a query, then periodically polling the service for changes. This is a bit of a hack, and typically the operators in charge of the service you're polling won't thank you for it.

So, this replayable log–based approach has two primary benefits. First, it makes it easy to react to events that are happening now, with a toolset specifically designed for manipulating them. Second, it provides a central repository that can push whole datasets to wherever they may be needed. This is pretty useful if you run a global business with data centers spread around the world, need to boot- strap or prototype a new project quickly, do some ad hoc data exploration, or build a complex service ecosystem that can evolve freely and independently. So there are some clear advantages to the event-driven approach (and there are of course advantages for the REST/RPC models too). But this is, in fact, only half the story. Streaming isn't simply an alternative to RPCs that happens to work better for highly connected use cases; it's a far more fundamental change in mindset that involves rethinking your business as an evolving stream of data

5.1 Use case for Real time

Activity tracking:

A website's users interact with frontend applications, which generate messages regarding actions the user is taking. This can be passive information, such as page views and click tracking, or it can be more complex actions, such as information that a user adds to their profile. The messages are published to one or more topics, which are then consumed by applications on the backend. These applications may be generating reports, feeding machine learning systems, updating search results, or performing other operations that are necessary to provide a rich user experience.

Messaging:

Real time Platform also used for messaging, where applications need to send notifications (such as emails) to users. Those applications can produce messages without needing to be concerned about formatting or how the messages will actually be sent. A single application can then read all the messages to be sent and handle them consistently, including:

• Formatting the messages (also known as decorating) using a common look and feel

• Collecting multiple messages into a single notification to be sent

• Applying a user's preferences for how they want to receive messages.

Metrics and logging:

Real time Platform is also ideal for collecting application and system metrics and logs. This is a use case in which the ability to have multiple applications producing the same type of message shines. Applications publish metrics on a regular basis to a topic, and those metrics can be consumed by systems for monitoring and alerting. They can also be used in an offline system like Hadoop to perform longer-term analysis, such as growth projections. Log messages can be published in the same way, and can be routed to dedicated log search systems like Elasticsearch or security analysis applications. Another feature of this platform is that when the destination system needs to change (e.g., it's time to update the log storage system), there is no need to alter the frontend applications or the means of aggregation.

Commit log:

Database changes can be published to Streaming Platform and applications can easily monitor this stream to receive live updates as they happen. This change log stream can also be used for replicating database updates to a remote system, or for consolidating changes from multiple applications into a single database view. Durable retention is useful here for providing a buffer for the change log, meaning it can be replayed in the event of a failure of the consuming applications. Alternatively, log-compacted topics can be used to provide longer retention by only retaining a single change per key.

Stream processing :

Another area that provides numerous types of applications is stream processing. While almost all usage of Real time messaging platforms can be thought of as stream processing, the term is typically used to refer to applications that provide similar functionality to map/reduce processing in Hadoop. Hadoop usually relies on aggregation of data over a long-time frame, either hours or days. Stream processing operates on data in real time, as quickly as messages are produced. Stream frameworks allow users to write small applications to operate on messages, performing tasks such as counting metrics, partitioning messages for efficient processing by other applications, or transforming messages using data from multiple sources.

5.2 Concepts of Publish/Subscribe Messaging:

Publish/subscribe messaging is a pattern that is characterized by the sender (publisher) of a piece of data (message) not specifically directing it to a receiver. Instead, the publisher classifies the message somehow, and that receiver (subscriber) subscribes to receive certain classes of messages. Pub/sub systems often have a broker, a central point where messages are published, to facilitate this.

How it Starts:

Many use cases for publish/subscribe start out the same way: with a simple message queue or inter-process communication channel. For example, you create an application that needs to send monitoring information somewhere, so you write in a direct connection from your application to an app that displays your metrics on a dash- board, and push metrics over that connection

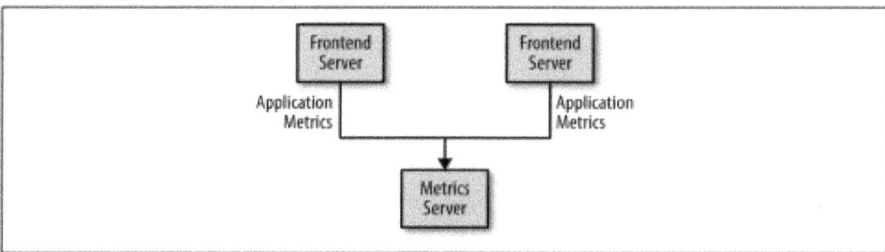

Fig 4.14 : A single direct metrics publisher

This is a simple solution to a simple problem that works when you are getting started with monitoring. Before long, you decide you would like to analyze your metrics over a longer term, and that doesn't work well in the dashboard. You start a new service that can receive metrics, store them, and analyze them. In order to support this, you modify your application to write metrics to both systems. By now you have three more applications that are generating metrics, and they all make the same connections to these two services. Your coworker thinks it would be a good idea to do active polling of the services for alerting as well, so you add a server on each of the applications to provide metrics on request. After a while, you have more applications that are using those servers to get individual metrics and use them for various purposes

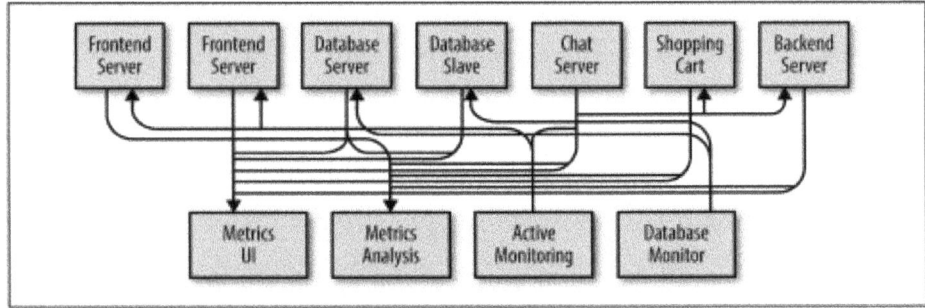

Fig 4.15 : Many metrics publishers, using direct connections

The technical debt built up here is obvious, so you decide to pay some of it back. You set up a single application that receives metrics from all the applications out there, and provide a server to query those metrics for any system that needs them. This reduces the complexity of the architecture

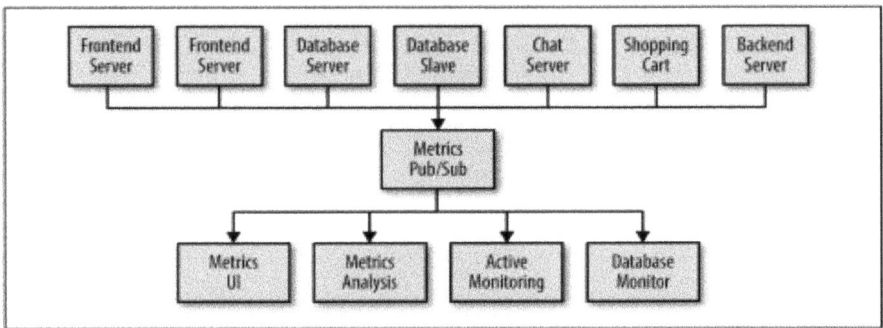

Fig 4.16: A Metrics Publish/ Subscribe Messaging System

At the same time that you have been waging this war with metrics, one of your co-workers has been doing similar work with log messages. Another has been working on tracking user behavior on the frontend website and providing that information to developers who are working on machine learning, as well as creating some reports for management. You have all followed a similar path of building out systems that decouple the publishers of the information from the subscribers to that information. This leads to many subsystems being built for your company. This refers to duplication. Your company is maintaining multiple systems for queuing data, all of which have their own individual bugs and limitations. You also know that there will be more use cases for messaging coming soon. There are many Pubsub Platforms available like Confluent Kafka, Solace, IBM MQ etc. In this book, I am writing about Kafka, but most of the concepts work on the Pub Sub Messaging that I talked about in above paragraph

5.3 Kafka –Real time PubSub Messaging Platform :

Apache Kafka is a publish/subscribe messaging system designed to solve this problem. It is often described as a "distributed commit log" or more recently as a "distributing streaming platform." A filesystem or database commit log is designed to provide a durable record of all transactions so that they can be replayed to consistently build the state of a system. Similarly, data within Kafka is stored durably, in order, and can be read deterministically. In addition, the data can be distributed within the system to provide additional protections against failures, as well as significant opportunities for scaling performance.

Messages and Batches :

The unit of data within Kafka is called a message. If you are approaching Kafka from a database background, you can think of this as similar to a row or a record. A message is simply an array of bytes as far as Kafka is concerned, so the data contained within it does not have a specific format or meaning to Kafka. A message can have an optional bit of metadata, which is referred to as a key. The key is also a byte array and, as with the message, has no specific meaning to Kafka. Keys are used when messages are to be written to partitions in a more controlled manner. The simplest such scheme is to generate a consistent hash of the key, and then select the partition number for that message by taking the result of the hash modulo, the total number of partitions in the topic. This assures that messages with the same key are always written to the same partition.

For efficiency, messages are written into Kafka in batches. A batch is just a collection of messages, all of which are being produced to the same topic and partition. An individual round trip across the network for each message would result in excessive over- head, and collecting messages together into a batch reduces this. Of course, this is a trade off between latency and throughput: the larger the batches, the more messages that can be handled per unit of time, but the longer it takes an individual message to propagate. Batches are also typically compressed, providing more efficient data trans- fer and storage at the cost of some processing power.

Schemas :

While messages are opaque byte arrays to Kafka itself, it is recommended that additional structure, or schema, be imposed on the message content so that it can be easily understood. There are many options available for message schema, depending on your application's individual needs. Simplistic systems, such as Javascript Object Notation (JSON) and Extensible Markup Language (XML), are easy to use and human-readable. However, they lack features such as robust type handling and compatibility between schema versions. Many Kafka developers favor the use of Apache Avro, which is a serialization framework originally developed for Hadoop. Avro provides a compact serialization format; schemas that are separate from the message pay- loads and that do not require code to be generated when they change; and strong data typing and schema evolution, with both backward and forward compatibility. A consistent data format is important in Kafka, as it allows writing and reading messages to be decoupled. When these tasks are tightly coupled, applications that sub- scribe to messages must be updated to handle the new data format, in parallel with the old format. Only then can the applications that publish the messages be updated to utilize the new format. By using well-defined schemas and storing them in a common repository, the messages in Kafka can be understood without coordination.

Topics and Partitions:

Messages in Kafka are categorized into topics. The closest analogies for a topic are a database table or a folder in a file System. Topics are additionally broken down into a number of partitions. Going back to the "commit log" description, a partition is a single log. Messages are written to it in an append-only fashion, and are read in order from beginning to end. Note that as a topic typically has multiple partitions, there is no guarantee of message time-ordering across the entire topic, just within a single partition. Figure 5.1shows a topic with four partitions, with writes being appended to the end of each one. Partitions are also the way that Kafka provides redundancy and scalability. Each partition can be hosted on a different server, which means that a single topic can be scaled horizontally across multiple servers to provide performance far beyond the ability of a single server.

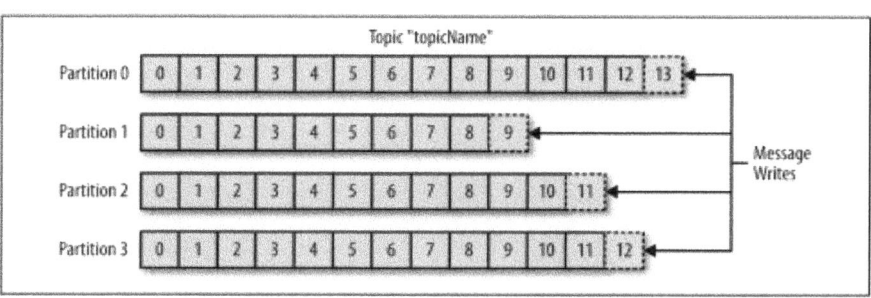

Fig 5.1: Topic with partitions

Kafka Producer : Writing message :

Whether you use Kafka as a queue, message bus, or data storage platform, you will always use Kafka by writing a producer that writes data to Kafka, a consumer that reads data from Kafka, or an application that serves both roles. For example, in a credit card transaction processing system, there will be a client application, perhaps an online store, responsible for sending each transaction to Kafka immediately when a payment is made. Another application is responsible for immediately checking this transaction against a rules engine and determining whether the transaction is approved or denied. The approve/deny response can then be written back to Kafka and the response can propagate back to the online store where the transaction was initiated. A third application can read both transactions and the approval status from Kafka and store them in a database where analysts can later review the decisions and perhaps improve the rules engine.

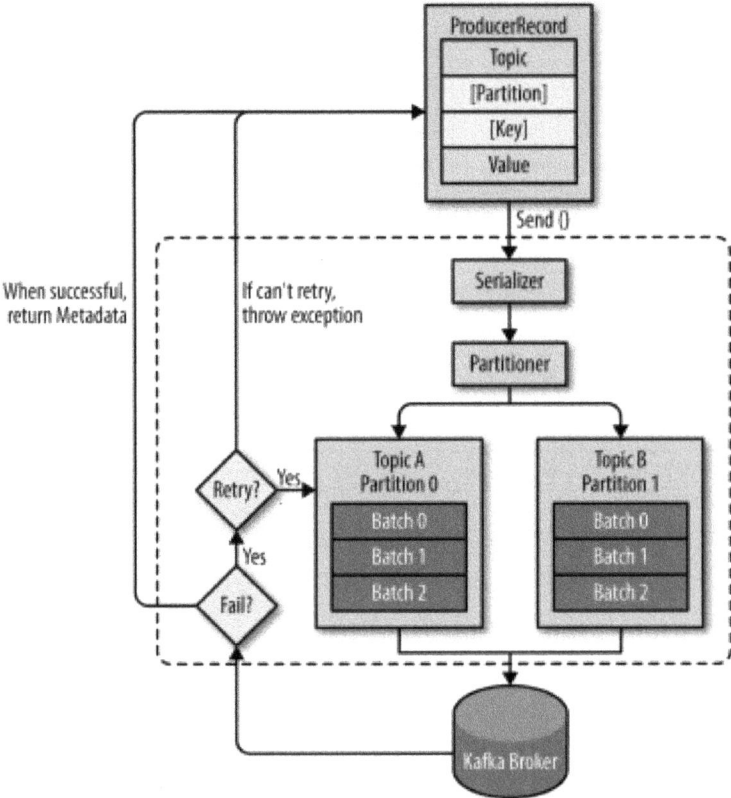

Fig 5.2: Kafka Producer Component

We start producing messages to Kafka by creating a Producer Record, which must include the topic we want to send the record to and a value. Optionally, we can also specify a key and/or a partition. Once we send the Producer Record, the first thing the producer will do is serialize the key and value objects to ByteArrays so they can be sent over the network. Next, the data is sent to a partitioner. If we specified a partition in the Producer Record, the partitioner doesn't do anything and simply returns the partition we specified. If we didn't, the partitioner will choose a partition for us, usually based on the Producer Record key. Once a partition is selected, the producer knows which topic and partition the record will go to. It then adds the record to a batch of records that will also be sent to the same topic and partition. A separate thread is responsible for sending those batches of records to the appropriate Kafka brokers. When the broker receives the messages, it sends back a response. If the messages were successfully written to Kafka, it will return a Record Metadata object with the Producer Overview, topic, partition, and the offset of the record within the partition. If the broker failed to write the messages, it will return an error. When the producer receives an error, it may retry sending the message a few more times before giving up and returning an error.

Kafka Consumers : Reading data from Topic

Applications that need to read data from Kafka use a Kafka Consumer to subscribe to Kafka topics and receive messages from these topics. Reading data from Kafka is a bit different than reading data from other messaging systems, and there are few unique concepts and ideas involved. Suppose you have an application that needs to read messages from a Kafka topic, run some validations against them, and write the results to another data store. In this case your application will create a consumer object, subscribe to the appropriate topic, and start receiving messages, validating them and writing the results. This may work well for a while, but what if the rate at which producers write messages to the topic exceeds the rate at which your application can validate them? If you are limited to a single consumer reading and processing the data, your application may fall further and further behind, unable to keep up with the rate of incoming messages. Obviously there is a need to scale consumption from topics. Just like multiple producers can write to the same topic, we need to allow multiple consumers to read from the same topic, splitting the data between them.

Kafka consumers are typically part of a consumer group. When multiple consumers are subscribed to a topic and belong to the same consumer group, each consumer in the group will receive messages from a different subset of the partitions in the topic. Let's take topic T1 with four partitions. Now suppose we created a new consumer, C1, which is the only consumer in group G1, and use it to subscribe to topic T1. Consumer C1 will get all messages from all four t1 partitions. If we add another consumer, C2, to group G1, each consumer will only get messages from two partitions. Perhaps messages from partition 0 and 2 go to C1 and messages from partitions 1 and 3 go to consumer C2. If G1 has four consumers, then each will read messages from a single partition

It is very common to have multiple applications that need to read data from the same topic. In fact, one of the main design goals in Kafka was to make the data produced to Kafka topics available for many use cases throughout the organization. In those cases, we want each application to get all of the messages, rather than just a subset. To make sure an application gets all the messages in a topic, ensure the application has its own consumer group. Unlike many traditional messaging systems, Kafka scales to a large number of consumers and consumer groups without reducing performance. In the previous example, if we add a new consumer group G2 with a single consumer, this consumer will get all the messages in topic T1 independent of what G1 is doing. G2 can have more than a single consumer, in which case they will each get a subset of partitions, just like we showed for G1, but G2 as a whole will still get all the messages regardless of other consumer groups.

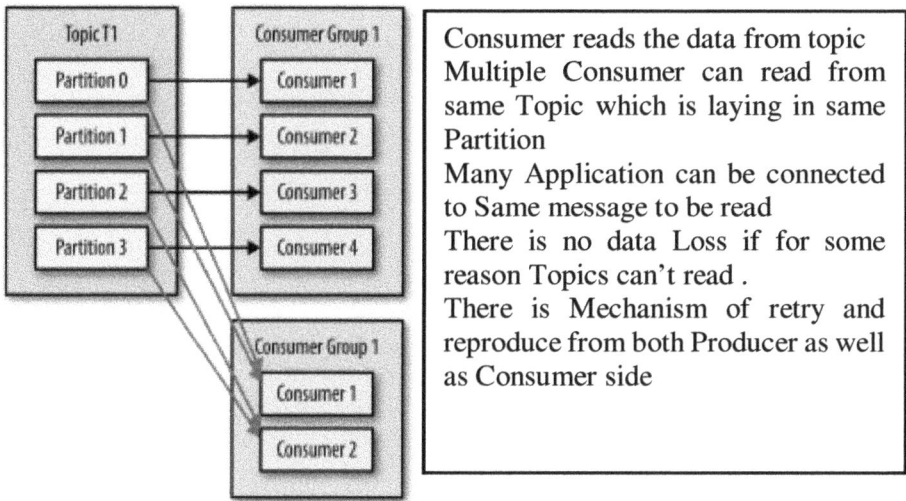

Consumer reads the data from topic
Multiple Consumer can read from same Topic which is laying in same Partition
Many Application can be connected to Same message to be read
There is no data Loss if for some reason Topics can't read .
There is Mechanism of retry and reproduce from both Producer as well as Consumer side

Figure 5.3 : Adding a new consumer group and Consumer Landscape

Chapter 6:
The BigSearch – Value of System records

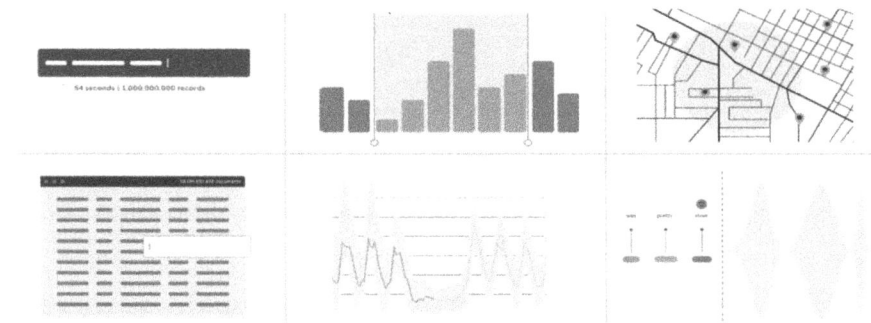

Fig 6.1: Search is Foundation to Data Access

The world is swimming in data. For years we have been simply overwhelmed by the quantity of data flowing through and produced by our systems. Existing technology has focused on how to store and structure warehouses full of data. That's all well and good—until you actually need to make decisions in real time informed by that data.

Most databases are astonishingly inept at extracting actionable knowledge from your data. Sure, they can filter by timestamp or exact values, but can they perform full-text search, handle synonyms, and score documents by relevance? Can they generate analytics and aggregations from the same data? Most importantly, can they do this in real time without big batch-processing jobs?

The system of Records is a key value point while it is fragmented and many source systems exist and organizations need to bring those systems as well as understand the records inside it. Hence Search is a key aspect to look at the data in speed.

6.1 Use Cases for Search:

- Wikipedia uses search capacity to provide full-text search with highlighted search snippets, and search-as-you-type and did-you-mean suggestions.

- The Guardian uses a search platform to combine visitor logs with social -network data to provide real-time feedback to its editors about the public's response to new articles.

- Stack Overflow combines full-text search with geolocation queries and uses more-like-this to find related questions and answers.

- GitHub uses search platform to query 130 billion lines of code

- Banks are required to address customer queries related to OTPs (One-Time Passwords) and SMS data through call center officers, particularly for regulatory purposes, dispute resolution, inaccessible data, and historical records. The SMS data volume amounts to 180 billion transactional records per year. Previously, the systems relied on Oracle-driven databases, which took 1-2 days to process these records. Call center officers are tasked with retrieving records in real-time to respond to customer queries. Similarly, regulatory subject matter experts (SMEs) need to extract data within minutes to provide it to regulatory authorities. This necessitates efficient text-based search capabilities, diverse dashboard views, and rapid search functionality.

- In the context of a bank's Loan Origination System (LOS), there is a need for deduplication and real-time search. Customers apply for various types of loans such as home loans, auto loans, personal loans, etc. Since these systems are typically set up independently, customers often secure loans without undergoing real-time eligibility verification. This can lead to issues in the collection process, as some customers may default on their loans. To address this challenge, real-time verification is essential, which involves employing various algorithms including phonetic checks, fuzzy logic, and text analytics to verify critical information such as Date of Birth (DOB), PAN (Permanent Account Number), Address, Aadhar, SSN (Social Security Number), and more.

- Building Relationships with Customer Data Objectives: Leverage anomaly detection and alerting to identify changes in purchasing behavior ✓ Correlate customer transaction data with additional data sets for analysis ✓ Understand customer demographics Data can be dynamically analyzed in new ways and additional datasets can be introduced to gain new insights about customers. With a deeper understanding of customer profiles, retailers can make informed decisions about where to open new stores or how to better localize their offerings

- Container and Orchestration Monitoring : Discover, collect, parse and index events as well as metrics to search and visualize ✓ Monitor logs and metrics from orchestration components and containers to identify and address infrastructural issues and optimize performance ✓ Correlate container data with application and host logs/metrics for a complete view Users can gain insight into the performance dynamics of their environment using familiar attributes like pod names or tags

- Insider Threat : Detect anomalies within the systems ✓ Correlate data from different systems (network, applications, physical) to identify threats ✓ Analyze communications for indicators of potential threat Insider actions, whether through intent, ignorance or error, are widely considered the greatest threat to information security

- Transaction Search & Analytics : Payments are growing and getting more complicated across channels , $320 Trillion Volume of Global Payments in 2025 in the form ACH, Wires, Real-time Payments, Bank Transfers, Checks, Cash, Cards, Mobile Payments, Digital Wallets, Embedded Payments, Payment Platforms, BNPL, QR Codes, Open Banking, etc. Customers demand secure, real-time access to their accounts with detailed analytics across ALL payment information to manage their business or personal assets.

- Customer 360 Applications: Build data profiles to offer greater personalization for online & offline channels. Unify records to build complete customer profiles. Enable custom search experiences for clients and employees. Empower service, sales teams, and marketers with the right insights to facilitate a more intimate customer journey. Elastic allows institutions to pull together data that references customer information, transactions, journeys, and preferences. Key ask is to √Offer tailored service to customers driven by their data profile √ Create new revenue opportunities for sales & marketing with bespoke content and solutions √Enable product & engineering leaders to develop solutions that meet customer needs √develop brand loyalty and build trust with customers

- Branch Banking & ATM Monitoring : The role of branch banking is changing but is still critical for traditional providers– helping to build relationships, provide tailored solutions, and solve more complex customer problems. However, a 'successful trip to the bank' requires all networks, applications, and services to be high-performing. A broken ATM, a slow network, or incomplete data profiles can hinder the journey. Is the bank open? Elastic enables financial institutions to ensure their customers and employees have reliable, high performing, and secure access to data and applications. Monitor ATMs, network performance and every endpoint at every branch. As soon as there is an issue, your ops team can reach out to that branch, schedule maintenance, new equipment, etc. - Reducing the friction for customers, branch employees, and management.

- Open Banking Visibility : 10.8 Billion Open banking API Calls by 2025 . The rise of Open Banking has created new opportunities, fueling the growth of Fintech, and granting more choice to retail and institutional customers, alike. Current adoption is accelerating. Open Banking channels need to be scalable and secure - capable of handling large volumes, while also reducing the risk of cyber-attacks and/or fraud events. We need a solution for Open Banking that solves Observability and Security features that prevent fraud and provide real-time business and SecOps analytics. Monitor your APIs to understand how they are being used by customers. Detects performance issues instantaneously. Enable security teams to protect against potential threats. Leverage embedded machine learning to enrich insights and spot irregularities. Have confidence in the deployment of new APIs, allowing your team to comply with local regulatory requirements.

- Hybrid Cloud Observability : Cloud migration is happening at a rapid pace across the banking industry - but the need to have hybrid environments will continue for the foreseeable future. The potential result is increased complexity and decreased visibility across IT ecosystems - especially if different logging and monitoring tools are being leveraged. We need to connect all telemetry data - traces, logs, and metrics to help you have better visibility into your hybrid ecosystem. Supports traditional monolithic applications as well as cloud-native and distributed micro services applications. Monitor and react to events happening anywhere in your environment and spot problems in real-time, so you don't have to wait for the answers. Leverage AIOps tools with machine learning to detect anomalies, then initiate corresponding actions or next steps. Empower SREs and developers to independently drive reliability, efficiency, and stability. Key Benefits Organization is looking ✓ Spend less time training analysts responsible for application monitoring ✓ Enable your team with the right tools, equipped with machine learning, to accelerate root-cause analysis ✓ Achieve faster detection times for issues and reduce MTTR✓ Boost Net Promoter Scores with faster, more reliable applications ✓Spend more time building new products and services instead of searching for and resolving issues

- Fraud Detection & Prevention: 89% Organizations Targets of fraud attack in 2025. As digital transformation progresses, bad actors are leveraging more sophisticated tools to facilitate fraud attacks. The expansion of payment types has increased blind spots and created challenges for fraud teams. In parallel, customer habits constantly change, making it more challenging to recognize anomalies and react quickly. We need a solution that enables financial providers to protect their customers by combining all data, across the enterprise, no matter the source, format, or location. With data in one place, it's available for analysis & detection in real-time. Elastic machine learning helps your team automatically detect anomalies, outliers from groups, and rare events. Utilize search technology on its own or alongside other solutions to improve speed of detection. Key Benefits Organization must be looking by Leverage alerts and collaboration tools to react quickly , Decrease false positives, enable a better customer journey, and generate insights that support the business and React, remediate, and prevent fraud at light speed

6.2 ElasticSearch :

One of the solutions I am refereeing is the search platform known as The ELK. This is a powerful software suite designed for log management and analysis. It's an acronym that represents the combination of three major components: Elasticsearch, Logstash, and Kibana. Each of these components plays a distinct role in helping organizations collect, store, analyze, and visualize large amounts of data, particularly logs and other time-series data, to gain valuable insights and make informed decisions.

1. **Elasticsearch**: Elasticsearch is a distributed, RESTful search and analytics engine built on top of the Apache Lucene library. It excels in full-text search and real-time data analysis. Elasticsearch can handle massive amounts of unstructured and structured data, making it ideal for logging and monitoring applications. It uses a JSON-based query language to search and retrieve data quickly. Elasticsearch's distributed nature ensures high availability, scalability, and fault tolerance.

2. **Logstash**: Logstash is a data collection pipeline tool that ingests, processes, and transforms data from various sources before sending it to Elastic search or other destinations. It can collect data from logs, metrics, event streams, databases, and more. Logstash allows users to define input plugins (data sources), filter plugins (data transformation), and output plugins (data destinations). This flexibility enables users to

clean, enrich, and structure incoming data before it's stored in Elasticsearch.

3. **Kibana**: Kibana is a powerful visualization and exploration tool that allows users to interact with the data stored in Elasticsearch. It provides a user-friendly web interface to create various visualizations such as charts, graphs, maps, and dashboards. Kibana enables users to explore and analyze data patterns, trends, and anomalies. With its user-driven approach, users can build custom dashboards and share them with others, making it an excellent tool for monitoring and analysis.

Elasticsearch is an open-source search engine built on top of Apache Lucene™, a full text search-engine library. Lucene is arguably the most advanced, high-performance, and fully featured search engine library in existence today—both open source and proprietary. But Lucene is just a library. To leverage its power, you need to work in Java and to integrate Lucene directly with your application. Worse, you will likely require a degree in information retrieval to understand how it works. Lucene is very complex. Elasticsearch is also written in Java and uses Lucene internally for all of its indexing and searching, but it aims to make full-text search easy by hiding the complexities of Lucene behind a simple, coherent, RESTful API. However, Elasticsearch is much more than just Lucene and much more than "just" full-text search. It can also be described as A distributed real-time document store where every field is indexed and searchable , It has Capable of scaling to hundreds of servers and petabytes of structured and unstructured data And it packages up all this functionality into a standalone server that your application can talk to via a simple RESTful API, using a web client from your favorite programming language, or even from the command line. It is easy to get started with Elastic search. It ships with sensible defaults and hides complicated search theory away from beginners.

Introduction of Vector Search :

Elastic search is based on Vector search, Advanced search technique. Vector search, also known as similarity search or nearest neighbor search, is an advanced search technique used to find items or data points in a dataset that are most similar or closely related to a given query item. Unlike traditional search methods that rely on exact matching or textual similarity, vector search leverages mathematical representations of data to perform similarity comparisons. This approach is particularly useful in various fields such as information retrieval, recommendation systems, image processing, natural language processing, and more.

How Vector Search Works: Vector search involves representing items in a dataset and query items as high-dimensional vectors in a multi-dimensional space. These vectors capture the inherent features and characteristics of the items. The similarity between two vectors is measured using mathematical metrics like cosine similarity, Euclidean distance, or other distance metrics. The goal is to find the vectors that are closest in the vector space to the query vector. In text-based applications, vector search can be used to find documents or articles that are semantically similar to a given query. This is particularly useful in content recommendation systems, where users are presented with articles, products, or other content that aligns with their preferences. For Image and Video Search, Vector search is extensively used in image and video processing. Images and videos are represented as vectors, and similar content can be retrieved quickly. This is vital in applications like reverse image search, content recommendation in visual media, and identifying duplicate or similar images. In NLP, vector search assists in finding documents or text passages that are contextually similar to a given query. It's used in chatbots, document clustering, and sentiment analysis. In bioinformatics, vector search helps identify similar protein sequences or DNA patterns, aiding in gene analysis and drug discovery.

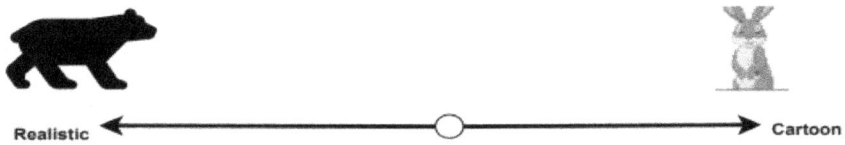

Fig 6.2: One Dimensional Vector: Embeddings represent your data

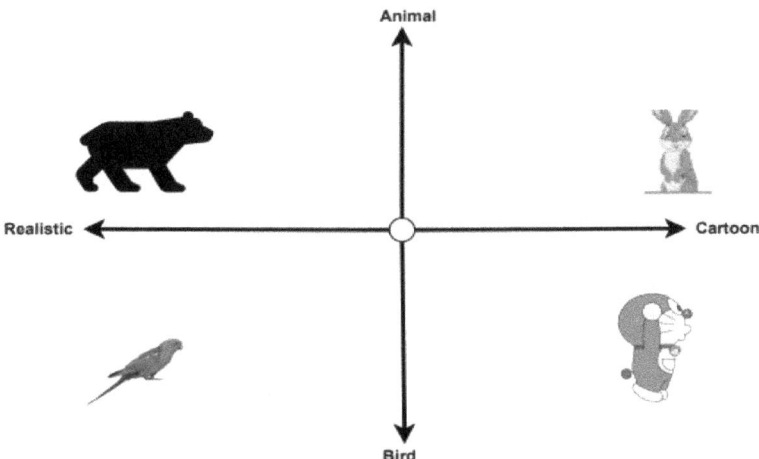

Fig 6.3: Multiple dimension represents different aspect of your data

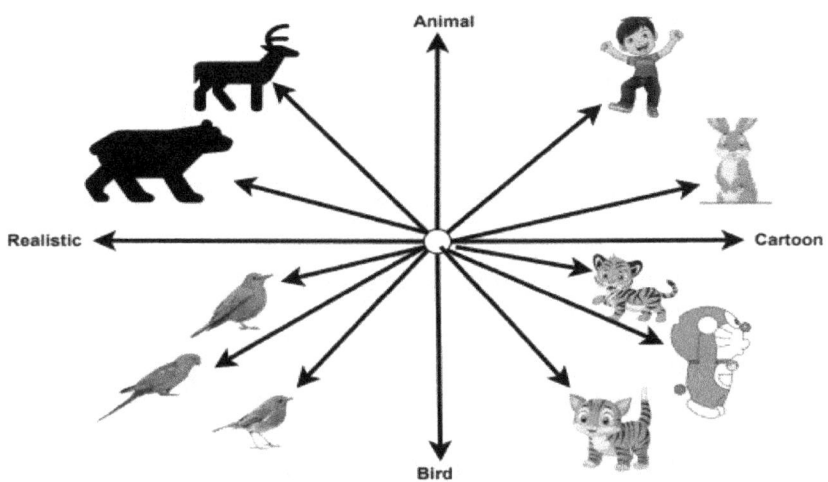

Fig 6.4: In embedded space, similar data are grouped

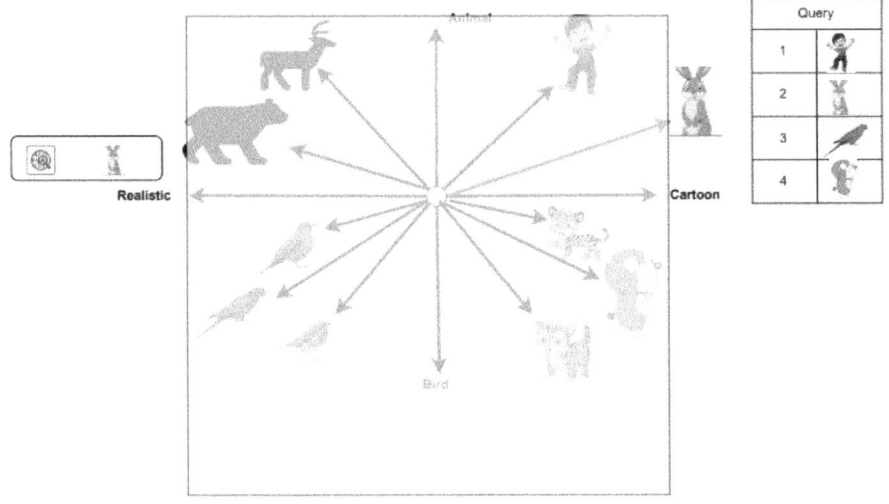

Fig 6.5: Vector search groups the elements

Vector search conceptual Architecture:

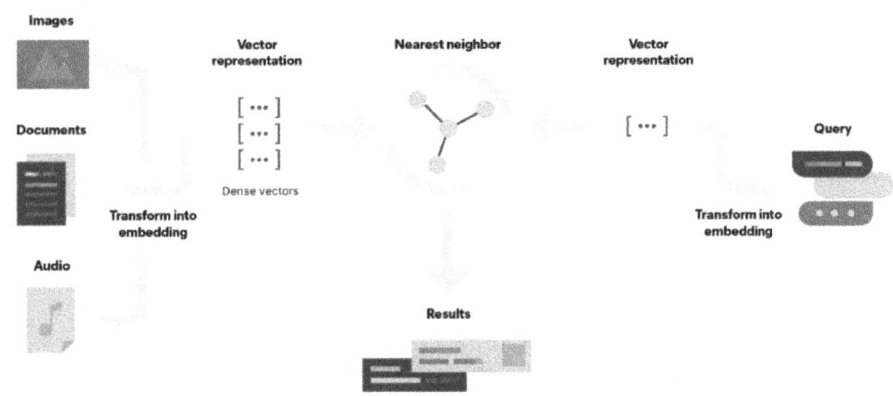

Fig 6.6: Architecture

6.2.1 How elastic search works:

1.Data Storage and Indexing: Elasticsearch integrates with various systems and brings the data in real or batch mode and stores the data in a distributed manner across multiple nodes (servers) within a cluster. Each node is responsible for storing a portion of the data and participating in search and indexing operations. Data is organized into indices, which can be thought of as collections of documents. A document is a JSON object that contains the actual data to be indexed and searched.

2. Inverted Index: Elasticsearch uses an inverted index, a data structure optimized for text search, to efficiently retrieve relevant documents. This index contains terms from the indexed documents along with references to the documents they appear in. This allows Elastic search to quickly locate documents containing specific terms, significantly speeding up search queries.

3. Document Analysis and Tokenization: When documents are indexed, Elastic search applies a process known as analysis. This involves tokenization, where documents are broken down into terms (words or tokens), and various normalization techniques, such as lowercasing, stemming, and removing stop words. These normalized terms are then stored in the inverted index, enhancing search accuracy.

4. Sharding and Replication: To ensure scalability and fault tolerance, Elasticsearch indexes are divided into smaller units called shards. Each shard is hosted on a separate node in the cluster. Sharding allows Elasticsearch to distribute data and search operations across multiple nodes, enabling parallel processing and accommodating larger datasets. Replication is used to create duplicate copies of shards (replicas) for redundancy and high availability.

5. Distributed Search: When a user submits a search query, Elasticsearch distributes the query across all relevant shards in the cluster. Each shard independently processes the query and returns relevant results. The results are then aggregated and ranked to provide the final set of search results.

6. RESTful API: Elasticsearch provides a RESTful API that allows users to interact with the system using HTTP methods like GET, POST, PUT, and DELETE. This API is used to perform various

operations, including indexing documents, searching for data, updating documents, managing indices, and more.

7. Distributed Coordination: Elasticsearch employs a distributed coordination mechanism to manage cluster state, handle node failures, and ensure data consistency across nodes. This coordination allows the cluster to adapt to changes in the cluster configuration and ensures that search and indexing operations can continue even if some nodes are unavailable.

8. Query DSL and Aggregations: Elasticsearch offers a Query DSL (Domain Specific Language) that allows users to construct complex search queries. Users can specify various criteria, filters, and sorting options to refine their search results. Additionally, Elasticsearch provides powerful aggregation capabilities, allowing users to summarize and analyze data to uncover insights.

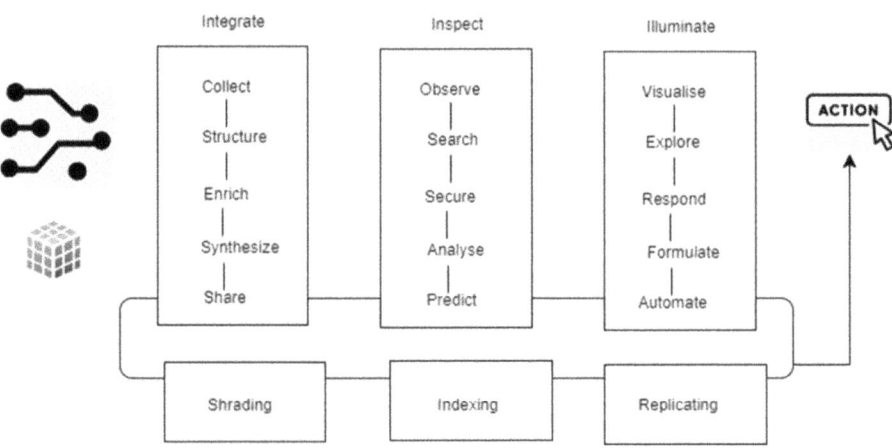

Fig 6.7 : How is the elastic Search works

6.3 Summary of Second Generation

In the era of digitalization, our world is inundated with data. Whether it's the digital traces we create online or the multitude of sensors capturing real-world events, the sheer magnitude of information produced on a daily basis is awe-inspiring. This data deluge has ushered in the era of "Big Data," a paradigm shift that has revolutionized our approach to understanding, managing, and harnessing information.

While traditional Data Warehouses typically handle several terabytes of data, in the realm of Big Data, we are dealing with petabytes of data. In our discussions, we have explored the fundamental concepts of Hadoop, Spark, and various internal mechanisms for managing the three Vs of data: volume, velocity, and variety.

Numerous platforms like Cloudera, Hortonworks, MapR, and IBM BigInsights, Cassendra, Graph Database Neo4j have a significant presence in this domain, with Cloudera being a prominent player. Just two years ago, Hortonworks merged with Cloudera, resulting in a unified entity that offers a wide array of Big Data functionalities.

Big Data Platforms empower data scientists with model-driven work capabilities, integrating numerous Spark Machine Learning libraries. The platform's features facilitate activities such as feature engineering, model building, experimentation, testing, and deployment. Moreover, it includes provisions for continuous model monitoring, retrofitting, and improvement."

When we build services using a streaming platform, some will be stateless—simple functions that take an input, perform a business operation, and produce an output. Some will be stateful, but read only, as in event-sourced views. Others will need to both read and write state, either entirely inside the Kafka ecosystem (and hence wrapped in Kafka's transactional guarantees), or by calling out to other services or databases. One of the most attractive properties of a stateful stream processing API is that all of these options are available, allowing us to trade the operational ease of stateless approaches for the data processing capabilities of stateful ones. There is also a mindset shift that comes with the streaming model, one that is inherently more asynchronous and adopts a more functional and data-centric style, when compared to the more procedural nature of traditional service interfaces.

Finally we talked about how Elasticsearch has not only reshaped the landscape of data search and analysis but also ignited a data exploration revolution. Its speed, scalability, and versatile querying capabilities have transformed how businesses glean insights from their information troves. As the world continues to produce an avalanche of data, Elasticsearch stands as a beacon, guiding organizations towards unlocking the hidden value within their data and facilitating informed decision-making in the digital age.

PART 3: Third Generation

Chapter 7: The Cloud DataPlatform

The history of cloud computing is marked by a progression from basic shared computing concepts to the highly sophisticated, diverse range of cloud services available today. As technology continues to evolve, cloud computing is likely to keep advancing and shaping the future of how businesses and individuals' access and use computing resources. 2006: Amazon Web Services (AWS) Launch, 2008: Google App Engine and Platform as a Service (PaaS), 2009: Microsoft Azure Launch are a few examples of Cloud generation.

The sharp increase in the adoption and popularity of cloud computing can be attributed to several key factors, driven by the technological, economic, and operational advantages it offers.

Cloud services offer the ability to easily scale computing resources up or down based on demand. This flexibility is particularly valuable for businesses dealing with fluctuating workloads, such as seasonal traffic spikes or rapid growth. Cloud services are accessible from anywhere with an internet connection, enabling remote work, collaboration, and access to applications and data on various devices. This has become especially important in the wake of the global shift to remote work due to the COVID-19 pandemic. Cloud platforms provide tools for rapid application deployment and development. Developers can provision resources quickly and focus on coding, reducing time-to-market for new products and services. Cloud providers offer a wide range of advanced services, including artificial intelligence, machine learning, big data analytics, and IoT capabilities. This empowers businesses to innovate, differentiate themselves, and create new revenue streams. Cloud services are available worldwide, enabling businesses to reach a global audience without having to set up physical data centers in multiple locations. Cloud providers optimize resource utilization, leading to better energy efficiency and reduced environmental impact compared to traditional data centers. AI is increasing sharply and needs a Cloud environment to do the job. Before we talk about various cloud platform, we should know what are use case that demands cloud

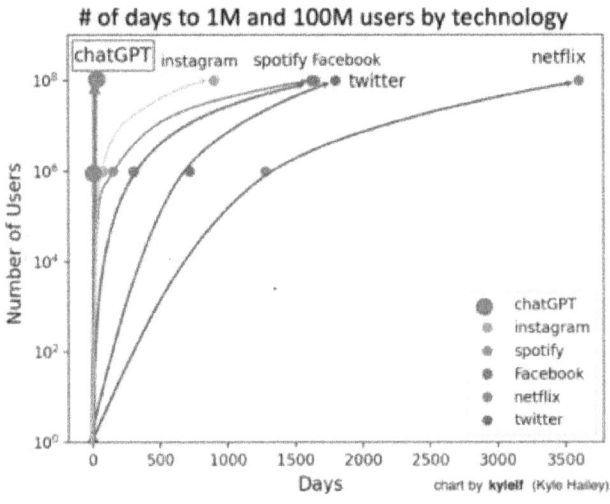

The cloud plays a crucial role in the development, deployment, and scalability of artificial intelligence (AI) solutions. It provides the infrastructure, tools, and resources necessary for AI development and enables organizations to harness the power of AI without the need for extensive hardware . Cloud enables GPU,TPU,ML/DL Services, Apis, IoT Integration, Cutting edge Tech Library

Fig 6.8: Unprecedented rapid adoption of AI and Cloud is key

7.1 Cloud Use Cases:

7.1.1 Real-Time Point-of-Sale Analytics in Supply Chain:

Disruptions in the supply chain — from reduced product supply and diminished warehouse capacity — coupled with rapidly shifting consumer expectations for seamless omnichannel experiences are driving retailers to rethink how they use data to manage their operations. Prior to the pandemic, 71% of retailers named lack of real-time visibility into inventory as a top obstacle to achieving their omnichannel goals. The pandemic only increased demand for integrated online and in-store experiences, placing even more pressure on retailers to present accurate product availability and manage order changes on the fly. Better access to real-time information is the key to meeting consumer demands in the new normal. In this blog, we'll address the need for real-time data in retail, and how to overcome the challenges of moving real-time streaming of point-of-sale data at scale with a data lakehouse.

The point-of-sale system:

The point-of-sale (POS) system has long been the central piece of in-store infrastructure, recording the exchange of goods and services between retailer and customer. To sustain this exchange, the POS typically tracks product inventories and facilitates replenishment as unit counts dip below critical levels. The importance of the POS to in-store operations cannot be overstated, and as the system of record for sales and inventory operations, access to its data is of key interest to business analysts.

Historically, limited connectivity between individual stores and corporate offices meant the POS system (not just its terminal interfaces) physically resided within the store. During off-peak hours, these systems might phone home to transmit summary data, which when consolidated in a data warehouse, provide a day-old view of retail operations performance that grows increasingly stale until the start of the next night's cycle.

Fig 7.1: Operational Cycle time

Modern connectivity improvements have enabled more retailers to move to a centralized, cloud-based POS system, while many others are developing near real-time integrations between in-store systems and the corporate back office. Near real-time availability of information means that retailers can continuously update their estimates of item availability. No longer is the business managing operations against their knowledge of inventory states as they were a day prior but instead is taking actions based on their knowledge of inventory states as they are now

Near real-time insights :

As impactful as near real-time insights into store activity are, the transition from nightly processes to continuous streaming of information brings particular challenges, not only for the data engineer, who must design a different kind of data processing workflow, but also for the information consumer. In this post, share some lessons learned from customers who've recently embarked on this journey and examine how key patterns and capabilities available through the lakehouse pattern can enable success

To illustrate this, consider a key challenge for many retail organizations today: the enablement of omni channel solutions. Such solutions, which enable buy-online, pickup in-store (BOPIS) and cross-store transactions, depend on reasonably accurate information about store inventory. If we were to limit our initial scope to this one need, the information requirements for our monitoring and analytics system become dramatically reduced. Once a real-time inventory solution is delivered and value is recognized by the business, we can expand our scope to consider other needs, such as promotions monitoring and fraud detection, expanding the breadth of information assets leveraged with each iteration.

Stages in POS:

POS systems are often not limited to just sales and inventory management. Instead, they can provide a sprawling range of functionality, including payment processing, store credit management, billing and order placement, loyalty program management, employee scheduling, time-tracking and even payroll, making them a veritable Swiss Army knife of in-store functionality. As a result, the data housed within the POS is typically spread across a large and complex database structure. If lucky, the POS solution makes a data access layer available, which makes this data accessible through more easily interpreted structures. But if not, the data engineer must sort through what can be an opaque set of tables to determine what is valuable and what is not. Regardless of how the data is exposed, the classic guidance holds true: identify a compelling business justification for your solution and use that to limit the scope of the information assets you initially consume. Such a justification often comes from a strong business sponsor, who is tasked with addressing a specific business challenge and sees the availability of more timely information as critical to their success,

Time Sensitivities:

Different processes generate data differently within the POS. Sales transactions are likely to leave a trail of new records appended to relevant tables. Returns may follow multiple paths, triggering updates to past sales records, the insertion of new, reversing sales records and/or the insertion of new information in returns specific structures. Vendor documentation, tribal knowledge and even some independent investigative work may be required to uncover exactly how and where event-specific information lands within the POS.

Understanding these patterns can help build a data transmission strategy for specific kinds of information. Higher frequency, finer-grained, insert-oriented patterns may be ideally suited for continuous streaming. Less frequent, larger-scale events may best align with batch-oriented, bulk data styles of transmission. But if these modes of data transmission represent two ends of a spectrum, you are likely to find most events captured by the POS fall somewhere in between. The beauty of the data lakehouse approach to data architecture is that multiple modes of data transmission can be employed in parallel. For data naturally aligned with the continuous transmission, streaming may be employed. For data better aligned with bulk transmission, batch processes may be used. And for those data falling in the middle, you can focus on the timeliness of the data required for decision-making and allow that to dictate the path forward. All of these modes can be tackled with a consistent approach to ETL implementation, a challenge that thwarted many earlier implementations of what were frequently referred to as Lambda Architecture

Land the data in stages :

Data arrives from the in-store POS systems with different frequencies, formats and expectations for timely availability. Leveraging the Bronze, Silver & Gold design pattern popular within lakehouses, you can separate initial cleansing, reformatting and persistence of the data from the more complex transformations required for specific business-aligned deliverables.

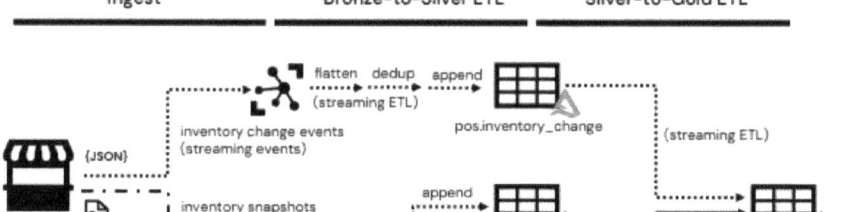

Fig 7.2 : POS Current Inventory using Bronze, Silver and Gold Pattern Data Persistence

All of this takes place in just the first few stages of maturation. In later stages, the organization's ability to detect meaningful signals within the stream may lead to more automated sense and response capabilities. Here, the highest levels of value in the data streams are unlocked. But monitoring and governance must be put into place and proven before the business will entrust its operations to these technologies

7.1.2 data lakes in the healthcare and life sciences industries :

A single patient produces approximately 80 megabytes of medical data every year. Multiply that across thousands of patients over their lifetime, and you're looking at petabytes of patient data that contains valuable insights. Unlocking these insights can help streamline clinical operations, accelerate drug R&D and improve patient health outcomes. But first, the data needs to be prepared for downstream analytics and AI. Unfortunately, most healthcare and life sciences organizations spend an inordinate amount of time simply gathering, cleaning and structuring their data. There are various challenges associated with Health care.

Volume: Scaling for rapid growing health Data

Genomics is perhaps the single best example of the explosive growth in data volume in healthcare. The first genome cost more than $1B to sequence. Given the prohibitive costs, early efforts (and many efforts still) focused on genotyping, a process to look for specific variants in a very small fraction of a person's genome, typically around 0.1%. That evolved to Whole Exome Sequencing, which covers the protein coding portions of the genome, still less than 2% of the entire genome. Companies now offer direct-to-consumer tests for Whole Genome Sequencing (WGS) that are less than $300 for 30x WGS. On a population level, the UK Biobank is releasing more than 200,000 whole genomes for research this year. It's not just genomics. Imaging, health wearable and electronic medical records are growing tremendously as well. Scale is the name of the game for initiatives like population health analytics and drug discovery. Unfortunately, many legacy architectures are built on-premises and designed for peak capacity. This approach results in unused compute power (and ultimately wasted dollars) during periods of low usage and doesn't scale quickly when upgrades are needed

Variety: Analyzing diverse health data

Healthcare and life sciences organizations deal with a tremendous amount of data variety, each with its own nuances. It is widely accepted that over 80% of medical data is unstructured, yet most organizations still focus their attention on data warehouses designed for structured data and traditional SQL-based analytics. Unstructured data includes image data, which is critical to diagnose and measure disease progression in areas like oncology, immunology and neurology (the fastest growing areas of cost), and narrative text in clinical notes, which are critical to understanding the complete patient health and social history. Ignoring these data types, or setting them to the side, is not an option. To further complicate matters, the healthcare ecosystem is becoming more interconnected, requiring stakeholders to grapple with new data types. For example, providers need claims data to manage and adjudicate risk-sharing agreements, and payers need clinical data to support processes like prior authorizations and to drive quality measures. These organizations often lack data architectures and platforms to support these new data types. Some organizations have invested in data lakes to support unstructured data and advanced analytics, but this creates a new set of issues. In this environment, data teams now need to manage two systems — data warehouses and data lakes — where data is copied across siloed tools, resulting in data quality and management issues

Velocity : Processing streaming data for real-time patient insights

In many settings, healthcare is a matter of life and death. Conditions can be very dynamic, and batch data processing — done even on a daily basis — often is not good enough. Access to the latest, up-to-the-second information is critical to successful interventional care. To save lives, streaming data is used by hospitals and national health systems for everything from predicting sepsis to implementing real-time demand forecasting for ICU beds. Additionally, data velocity is a major component of the healthcare digital revolution. Individuals have access to more information than ever before and are able to influence their care in real time. For example, wearable devices — like the continuous glucose monitors provided by Livongo — stream real-time data into mobile apps that provide personalized behavioral recommendations. Despite some of these early successes, most organizations have not designed their data architecture to accommodate streaming data velocity. Reliability issues and challenges integrating real-time data with historic data is inhibiting innovation.

Veracity : Building trust in healthcare data and AI

Last, but not least, clinical and regulatory standards demand the utmost level of data accuracy in healthcare. Healthcare organizations have high public health compliance requirements that must be met. Data democratization within organizations requires governance. Additionally, organizations need good model governance when bringing artificial intelligence (AI) and machine learning (ML) into a clinical setting. Unfortunately, most organizations have separate platforms for data science workflows that are disconnected from their data warehouse. This creates serious challenges when trying to build trust and reproducibility in AI-powered applications

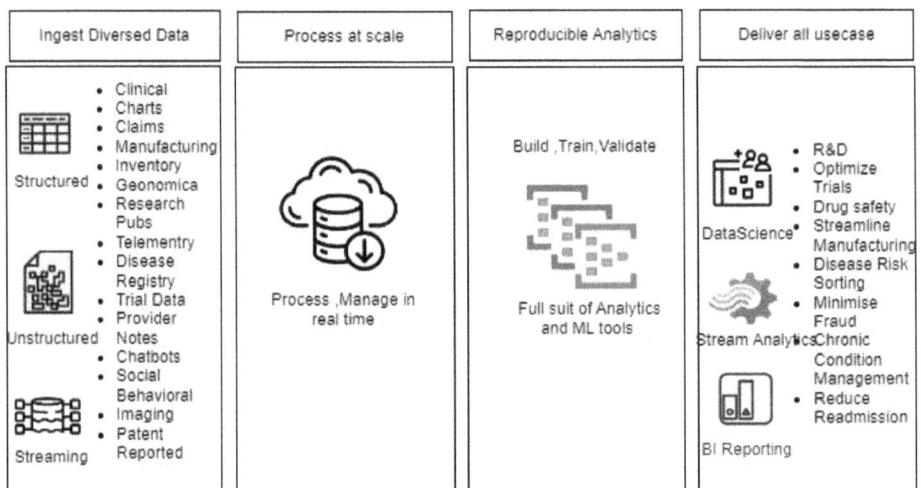

Fig 7.3: Architecture for Health Science

Banking Various Use Case:

The adoption of cloud computing in the banking sector is driving a fundamental shift in how financial services are delivered and managed. Banks that embrace cloud technologies stand to gain significant advantages in terms of cost savings, operational efficiency, customer experiences, and innovation. By leveraging cloud computing, the banking industry can position itself to meet the demands of the digital age and offer enhanced services to customers in a rapidly changing financial landscape.

7.1.3 Regulatory Reporting with timeless and reliability delivery:

Managing risk and regulatory compliance is an increasingly complex and costly endeavor. Regulatory change has increased 500% since the

2008 global financial crisis and boosted the regulatory costs in the process. Given the fines associated with non-compliance and SLA breaches (banks hit an all-time high in fines of $10 billion in 2019 for AML), processing reports has to proceed even if data is incomplete. On the other hand, a track record of poor data quality is also fined because of "insufficient controls." As a consequence, many financial services institutions (FSIs) are often left battling between poor data quality and strict SLAs, balancing between data reliability and data timeliness. One of the cloud platforms provided by Databrick is Delta Live Tables that guarantee the acquisition and processing of regulatory data in real time to accommodate regulatory SLAs. With Delta Sharing and Delta Live Tables combined, analysts gain real-time confidence in the quality of regulatory data being transmitted. FIRE Data Model is being used in most Financial Regulatory Reporting.

FIRE Data Model :

The Financial Regulatory data standard (FIRE) defines a common specification for the transmission of granular data between regulatory systems in finance. Regulatory data refers to data that underlies regulatory submissions, requirements and calculations and is used for policy, monitoring and supervision purposes. The FIRE data standard is supported by the European Commission, the Open Data Institute and the Open Data Incubator FIRE data standard for Europe via the Horizon 2020 funding program. As part of this solution, we contributed a PySpark module that can interpret FIRE data models into Apache Spark™ operating pipelines

Fig 7.4: Fire Data Model Standard

Delta Live table:

Delta Live Tables, which makes it easy to build and manage reliable data pipelines at enterprise scale. With the ability to evaluate multiple expectations, discard or monitor invalid records in real time, the benefits of integrating the FIRE data model on Delta Live Tables are obvious. As illustrated in the following architecture, Delta Live Tables will ingest granular regulatory data landing onto cloud storage, schematize content and validate records for consistency in line with the FIRE data specification. Keep reading to see us demo the use of Delta Sharing to exchange granular information between regulatory systems in a safe, scalable and transparent manner

Enforcing Schema:

Even though some data formats may "look" structured (e.g., JSON files), enforcing a schema is not just a good engineering practice; in enterprise settings, and especially in the space of regulatory compliance, schema enforcement guarantees any missing field to be expected, unexpected fields to be discarded and data types to be fully evaluated (e.g., a date should be treated as a date object and not a string). It also proof-tests your systems for eventual data drift. Using the FIRE PySpark module, we can programmatically retrieve the Spark schema required to process a given FIRE entity (collateral entity in that example) that we apply on a stream of raw records

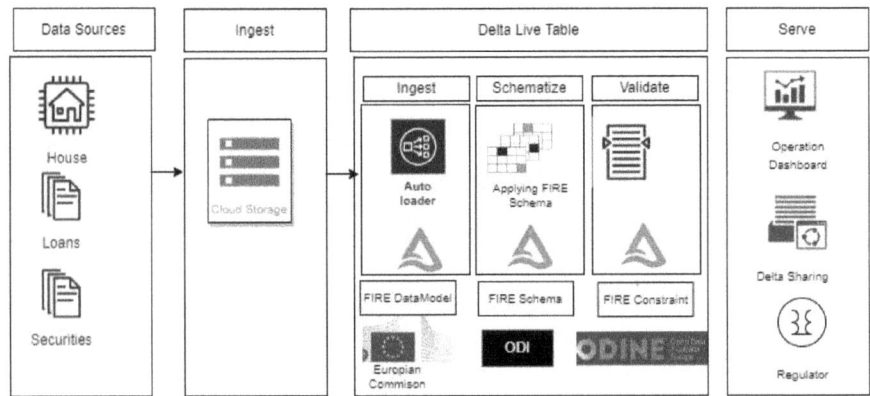

Fig 7.5: Design of flow using Delta Live Tables

Transmission of Regulatory Data :

With full confidence in both data quality and volume, financial institutions can safely exchange information between regulatory systems using Delta Sharing, an open protocol for enterprise data exchange. Not constraining end users to the same platform nor relying on complex ETL pipelines to consume data (accessing data files through an SFTP server, for instance), the open- source nature of Delta Lake makes it possible for data consumers to access schematized data natively from Python, Spark or directly through MI/BI dashboards (such as Tableau or Power BI). Although we could be sharing our silver table as is, we may want to use business rules that only share regulatory data when a predefined data quality threshold is met. In this example, we clone our silver table at a different version and to a specific location segregated from our internal networks and accessible by end users (DMZ). Many DaaS (Data as a Service) solution could be plugged to access the data

7.1.4 AML –Key Problem of Bank to stand tall against Crime:

Anti-money laundering (AML) compliance has been undoubtedly one of the top agenda items for regulators providing oversight of financial institutions across the globe. As AML evolved and became more sophisticated over the decades, so have the regulatory requirements designed to counter modern money laundering and terrorist financing schemes. The Bank Secrecy Act of 1970 provided guidance and framework for financial institutions to put in proper controls to monitor financial transactions and report suspicious fiscal activity to relevant authorities. This law provided the framework for how financial institutes combat money laundering and financial terrorism

Current AML operations bear little resemblance to those of the last decade. The shift to digital banking, with financial institutions (FIs) processing billions of transactions daily, has resulted in the ever-increasing scope of money laundering, even with stricter transaction monitoring systems and robust Know Your Customer (KYC) solutions.

Building AML Solutions in DataLake :

The operational burden of processing billions of transactions a day comes from the need to store the data from multiple sources and power intensive, next-gen AML solutions. These solutions provide powerful risk analytics and reporting while supporting the use of advanced machine learning models to reduce false positives and improve downstream investigation efficiency. FIs have already taken steps to solve the infrastructure and scaling problems by moving from on premises to cloud for better security, agility and the economies of scale required to store massive amounts of data. But then there is the issue of how to make sense of the massive amounts of structured and unstructured data collected and stored on cheap object storage. While cloud vendors provide an inexpensive way to store the data, making sense of the data for downstream AML risk management and compliance activities starts with storage of the data in high-quality and performant formats for downstream consumption.

On top of the data storage challenges outlined above, AML analysts face some key domain-specific challenges:

• Improve time-to-value parsing unstructured data such as images, textual data and network links

• Reduce DevOps burden for supporting critical ML capabilities such as entity resolution, computer vision and graph analytics on entity metadata

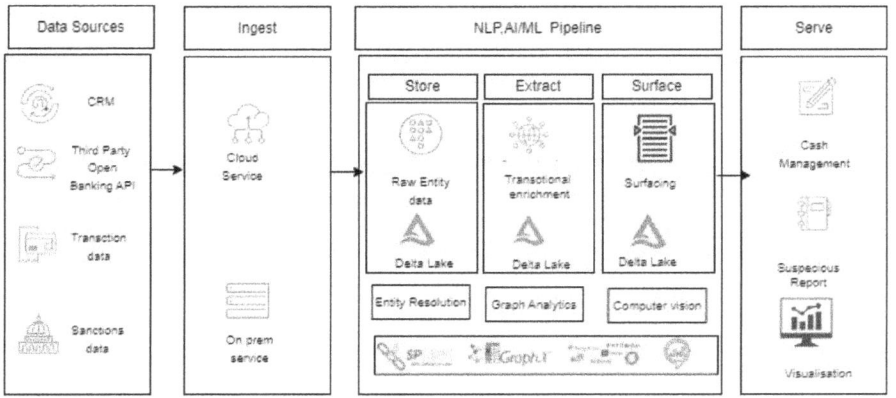

Fig 7.6: Architecture for AML workload

AML Patterns with Graph capabilities:

One of the main data sources that AML analysts use as part of a case is transaction data. Even though this data is tabular and easily accessible with SQL, it becomes cumbersome to track chains of transactions that are three or more layers deep with SQL queries. For this reason, it is important to have a flexible suite of languages and APIs to express simple concepts such as a connected network of suspicious individuals transacting illegally together. Luckily, this is simple to accomplish using Graph Frames, a graph API solves it.

Scenario 1 — synthetic identities:

As mentioned above, the existence of synthetic identities can be a cause for alarm. Using graph analysis, all of the entities from our transactions can be analyzed in bulk to detect a risk level. In our analysis, this is done in three phases:

• Based on the transaction data, extract the entities

• Create links between entities based on address, phone number or email

• Use GraphFrames-connected components to determine whether multiple entities (identified by an ID and other attributes above) are connected via one or more links Based on how many connections (i.e., common attributes) exist between entities, we can assign a lower or higher risk score and create an alert based on high-scoring groups. Below is a basic representation of this idea

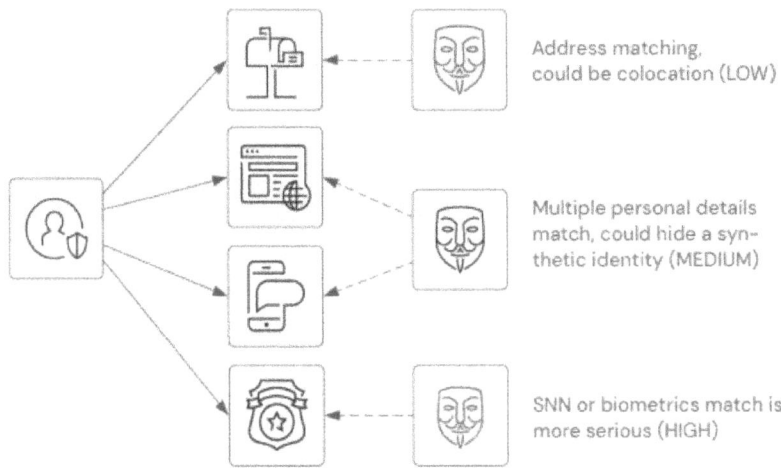

Based on how many connections (i.e., common attributes) exist between entities, Assign a lower or higher risk score and create an alert based on high-scoring groups

Fig 7.7: Matching Models

Scenario 2 — Structuring

Another common pattern is called structuring, which occurs when multiple entities collude and send smaller "under the radar" payments to a set of banks, which subsequently route larger aggregate amounts to a final institution (as depicted below on the far right). In this scenario, all parties have stayed under the $10,000 threshold amount, which would typically alert authorities. Not only is this easily accomplished with graph analytics, but the motif finding technique can be automated to extend to other permutations of networks and locate other suspicious transactions in the same way.

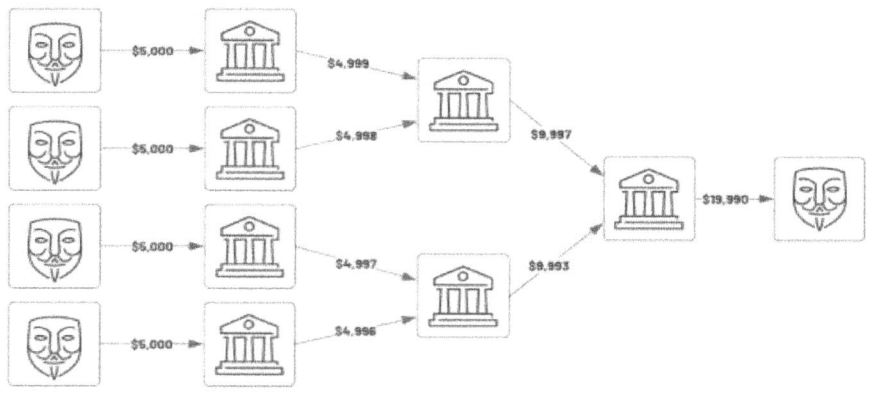

Fig 7.8 : Multiple entities collude

Scenario 3 — Risk score propagation:

The identified high-risk entities will have an influence (a network effect) on their circle. So, the risk score of all the entities that they interact with must be adjusted to reflect the zone of influence. Using an iterative approach, we can follow the flow of transactions to any given depth and adjust the risk scores of others affected in the network. As mentioned previously, running graph analytics avoids multiple repeated SQL joins and complex business logic, which can impact performance due to memory constraints. Graph analytics and Pregel API was built for that exact purpose. Initially developed by Google, Pregel allows users to recursively "propagate" messages from any vertex to its corresponding neighbors, updating vertex state (their risk score here) at each step. We can represent our dynamic risk approach using Pregel API as follows.

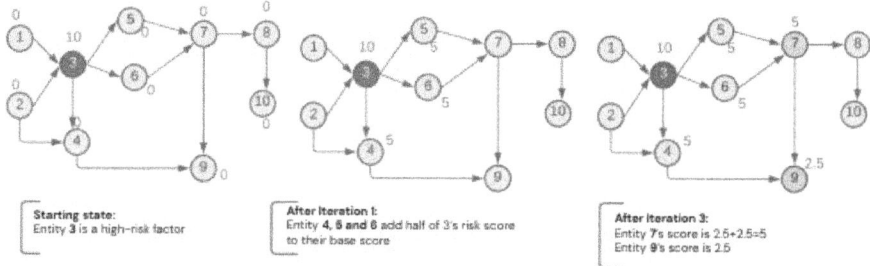

Fig 7.9: Risk Score varies with iteration

7.1.5 Elevating Customer Engagement Through Personalized Experiences

In the era of data-driven decision-making and heightened customer expectations, businesses are constantly seeking innovative ways to enhance customer engagement and loyalty. One such approach that has gained significant attention is "Hyper personalization." Hypersonalization goes beyond traditional personalization strategies by leveraging advanced technologies and data analytics to create deeply individualized experiences for customers. This approach aims to anticipate and fulfill customer needs and preferences on an unprecedented level.

Amazon is a prime example of a company that has mastered the art of personalization to create a seamless and highly tailored shopping experience for its customers. The story of Amazon's personalization journey is a testament to how data-driven insights and advanced technologies can revolutionize e-commerce and customer engagement. Amazon earns 10.2 billion Dollar, Starbuck earn $1 Billion from their Personalization Program per year

Typical process Amazon follows as per below.

1. Customer-Centric Approach: Amazon's personalization journey began with its founder, Jeff Bezos, emphasizing a customer-centric philosophy. The company's mission to be the "Earth's most customer-centric company" laid the foundation for its focus on understanding and meeting individual customer needs.

2. Data Collection and Analysis: From its inception, Amazon collected vast amounts of data on customer interactions, purchase history, browsing behavior, and preferences. The company used this data to gain insights into individual shopping habits, enabling them to make informed decisions about how to personalize the shopping experience.

3. Recommendations Engine: One of Amazon's most well-known personalization features is its recommendation engine. The "Customers

who bought this also bought" and "Recommended for you" sections leverage collaborative filtering algorithms to suggest products based on a customer's past purchases and the purchasing behavior of similar customers.

4. Dynamic Pricing: Amazon uses dynamic pricing algorithms that take into account factors like demand, competitor prices, and customer preferences. This enables the company to offer personalized prices to different customers, maximizing revenue and offering competitive prices.

5. Personalized Emails and Notifications: Amazon sends personalized email recommendations to customers, reminding them of products they viewed, left in their cart, or might be interested in based on their purchase history. This gentle reminder encourages customers to return to the platform and complete their purchase.

6. One-Click Ordering: Amazon's patented "One-Click" ordering system simplifies the checkout process, enabling customers to make purchases with a single click. This frictionless experience is based on the understanding that minimizing steps in the purchasing journey can increase conversion rates.

7. Amazon Prime and Content Personalization: Amazon Prime offers personalized benefits, including expedited shipping, streaming services, and exclusive deals. Additionally, Amazon's content platforms, like Amazon Prime Video and Kindle, use personalized recommendations to suggest movies, TV shows, and books based on customer preferences.

Understanding Personalization in Banking:

Personalization is about crafting experiences that resonate with customers on a one-to-one basis. It involves tailoring every interaction, message, and recommendation to align with an individual's unique characteristics, behaviors, and context. While personalization aims to segment audiences and offer relevant content, Personalization takes it further by creating experiences that are almost predictive, enhancing customer satisfaction and loyalty. With more and more people opting for contactless payment options because of the global pandemic, there has been a steep surge in the growth of digital payment apps industry. With the tailwinds in digital payments, it's becoming increasingly important to deliver a seamless payment experience to users across the funnel.

Personalization Framework :

Before we put the framework, we must categories the Customer DNA and other activities into our guiding principle. Below is high level classification:

Customer DNA – Age, Gender, Geography, Life stage, Income, Occupation and Product Behavior – Balance, utilization, ADB, AUM, Spend with Customer events like life stage events – Marriage, birth of child etc

Interest Shown- Application Started, submitted etc, Feedback that captures recorded the service products with having many external Bureau, trade line data etc. There are many personas related to affluent, digital Native Metro, Self-employed digital transactor, Young School going, Gen Z, Old Age

Below are set of nudges for reference

1. While onboarding users, nudge them to add their bank account details for quick transactions.
2. Nudge users to explore different features of your app – payment of utility bills like electric bills, mobile
3. Prompt users to complete their KYC.
4. Nudge users to make UPI transactions by highlighting rewards/cashback on making payments
5. Nudge users to claim rewards/unlock bonuses on bill payments.
6. Nudge users to check out the voucher options/discounts available on various payment methods.

7. Highlight the 'send money' option.
8. Deploy reminder nudges for recharges and bill payments to avoid late charges.
9. Nudge users to set monthly reminders for various payments.
10. Nudge users to top-up their wallet for quick payments.
11. Users who use their credit cards often, nudge them to check out their credit card scores.
12. Show a walkthrough that guides users to explore the various policy options on your app. Deploy a series of nudges that starts with getting the users' attention to the policy option button followed by a nudge on the option to know/learn more about the policy and finally prompt users to calculate the premium on the chosen policy.
13. For users who already have an active policy, nudge them to renew their policy (maybe 7 days before the renewal date). Depending upon the user behavior, surface relevant policy options – healthcare, car, etc.
15. Nudge users to borrow money. – 'Low on money? Borrow some'.
16. Nudge users to keep a track of their score.
17. Guide users through the loan application process by deploying a walkthrough.
18. Guide users to complete their loan application if they have dropped off midway.
19. Nudge users to set reminders to pay monthly installments.
20. Deploy a walkthrough to drive the user's attention to key features like pricing, portfolio, etc.
21. Nudge users to check out the trading guide.
22. Nudge users to bookmark/add coins to the watchlist.
23. When a user has browsed through Exchange but not yet bought any coins, show a nudge on the currency with "X users have bought BTC in the last 7 hours".

24. Mutual fund, Equity fund like your friend

25. Asset loans, Investment plan like your friend

Monetizing upon user's actions and intent to engage with your app, planting these nudges across the app helps in better onboarding, increases the policies' purchase, boosts cross-selling and upselling, and increases policy renewal.

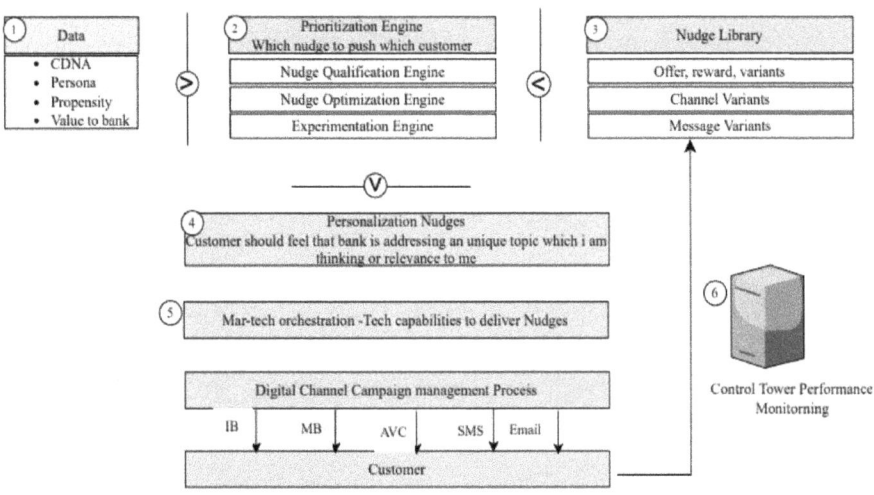

Fig 7.10 : 6 Key Pillars of Nudge framework

7.1.6 How to solve the Broken Customer Experience with Customer 360 degree:

In the ever-evolving and fiercely competitive landscape of the banking industry, delivering an exceptional customer experience is of paramount importance. Banks offer a diverse array of products and services, each playing a pivotal role in meeting the financial needs of their customers. However, a range of challenges, including difficulties in onboarding, service disruptions, accessibility issues, and communication breakdowns, can result in dissatisfied customers and potentially harm the bank's reputation. To effectively address these challenges and truly prioritize customer satisfaction, banks must concentrate on several critical areas.

Banks offer a multitude of products and services, such as CASA accounts, loans, credit cards, merchant acquiring systems, wholesale banking, and digital banking, all of which cater to customers' diverse banking requirements. Unfortunately, there are instances where onboarding processes for products like CASA, loans, and credit cards encounter failures. Accessibility and processing issues, such as login problems for internet and mobile banking, can also disrupt customer experiences. Servicing journeys, whether ticket-based or not, along with inbound and outbound communications, may frequently face disruptions.

Moreover, inundating customers with excessive marketing messages that lack relevance can have a detrimental impact. Such practices can lead to a deterioration in the overall customer experience, prompting customers to voice their frustrations on social platforms. It is crucial to resolve ombudsman complaints promptly and effectively to truly prioritize and achieve a customer-centric approach, often referred to as 'customer obsession'.

Scenario : Customer is trying to pay the credit card and his flow process

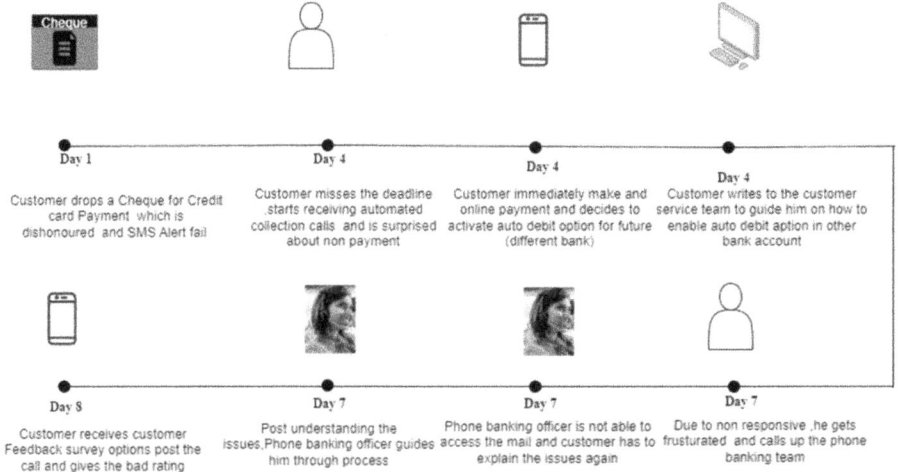

Fig 7.11: Customer Service journey for Credit card

Solution with below options to handle the customer Challenge and ask to build the Enterprise approach.

Institutional Memory, 360 view and Seamless Interactions with Continuity

- Appropriate Narrative/Scripts for interactions (ticket and non- ticket based)
- Incorporating past feedback & Status
- Recommend next best actions to aid intelligent conversion

Cross Channel Portability

- Act as an Orchestration Layer for enabling Continuity of failed on boarding and servicing journey
- Seamless transition between channels like IB/MB/OCC (Outgoing Call center), WhatsApp, Social site (LinkedIn, Twitter, Facebook, etc)

Feedback loop and Personalization for Continuous Improvement

- Feedback from Customers on Interactions
- NPS Feedback loop closure for valuable Customers
- Continuous Improvement basis feedback loop

Further compartmental of above 3 Principle into more action oriented, below Points are considered as initial identification that goes as scope of this paragraph

Omni 360 (Next best Action) –We will manage various metrics including FCR (First Contact Resolution), Frontline Productivity, Number of Complaints, Complaint Resolution Time (TAT), and NPS (Net Promoter Score). Customers will not need to reiterate the details of their interactions across different bank channels when they contact the Customer Center because their information is already accessible.

Application Tracker for on boarding & Service Journey –We will address various Key Result Areas (KRAs) including the number of complaints (4,000 per month), status inquiries (1,75,000 per month), customer verbatim feedback (18% from the bottom 2 categories), development efforts, and NPS (Net Promoter Score). This approach aims to enhance transparency and provide real-time updates on the end-to-end application status, eliminating the need for follow-up calls to check progress. We will also actively track incomplete customer journeys

Proactive Support for breaching service guarantee – Many Burgundy and H1N Customer Metrics NPS will be taken care. Proactive Communication in case of non-resolution for this segment customer.

Cross Channel Portability for CASA (Current Account/Savings Account) on boarding – Digital journey provides customers to open their account without physically going to the bank. This is additional channel and should not work silo

Cross Channel Portability of Serving Journey – Multiple service journey platforms, such as IB, MB, Avaya, Genesys, CRM, and CMS, must be seamlessly interconnected. We will address metrics related to duplicate information, incorrect tagging, and customer handling to ensure smooth cross-portability across these platforms

Predictive Ombudsman Complaints - By leveraging AI/ML technology on social data combined with in-house data, we can deliver predictive insights. Self-service capabilities will facilitate a deeper understanding of customer issues and concerns, allowing for swift resolution without the need for extensive data collection. The model will extract existing data points to provide actionable insights for problem-solving

Cross Channel Portability for Cards on Boarding Journeys – Customers often encounter challenges when applying for various types of cards, such as Credit, Debit, Flipkart, Fuel, or Priority Pass cards, at banks. The process is often cumbersome, involving extensive documentation, verification steps, and manual processes. Additionally, human intervention can lead to inconsistencies and negatively impact the overall customer onboarding experience. Currently, multiple channels exist for customers to acquire cards, but when a disconnect occurs between these channels, customers often contact the call center for assistance, which may not always provide a satisfactory solution. The customer service officer may also face challenges due to the multitude of channels, and the lack of collaboration among these channels further complicates the situation

Cross Channel Portability for Loans – A similar scenario unfolds when customers seek various types of loans, such as Auto, Home, Credit Card, Personal, Gold, or educational loans. For instance, a customer sitting in a Tanishq Gold shop eagerly awaits an OTP to log in for a gold loan application. The anticipation of obtaining the loan and leaving with their desired gold can be a joyful experience. However, sometimes, the OTP doesn't arrive, leading to a disappointing customer experience, even when they started their visit to the gold shop in high spirits.

Close Looping on CX Survey issues raised – Customer Survey Link goes to customer to share his feedback. Many times, the voice heard from Customer won't be taken up or won't stitch with another system, Hence Survey becomes tissue paper. This must be free flowing information with all system and get it served automatically

Personalization for Frontline/Customers – Generic Message/Information is no more profitable place for either Frontline officer or Customer. It took a lot of time for frontline workers to solve Customer challenges while Customer is in waiting mode, similarly when Personalized message goes to customer with his service/Complaints, Customer gets delighted. Hence, Relevance is key and it should be customer centria.

Solution Diagram:

We aim to centralize data from diverse core systems within a 'Data Lake.' This repository encompasses a vast array of information, including transactional records, service requests, rejections, transcripts, and alternative data sourced from various bureaus, alongside geographical data. In numerous banking institutions, a complex ecosystem comprises more than 150 systems, with over 40 of them holding pivotal roles in managing customer-related data. This customer-centric data frequently contains personally identifiable information (PII) and sensitive personal data and information (SPDI), necessitating strict compliance with regulatory constraints.

Numerous technological components, including modern tools such as Cloud, Micro Services, AI/Deep Learning, and Big Data, will be employed for data scraping, engineering, and text analytics. These technologies will support the aggregation of comprehensive information for a 360-degree view accessible to customers when they raise queries with call center officers or through self-service portals, depending on their access privileges.

The expected data volume will be substantial, encompassing various formats like structured, unstructured, video, and audio. Handling this data will require complex parsing techniques. The Integration Layer, as previously described, will facilitate the seamless flow of data between systems.

At the forefront, the Engagement Layer plays a pivotal role in connecting with customers and facilitating interactions. It caters to customers across various channels, ensuring real-time access to all the information they require by internally connecting with the bank's entire system.

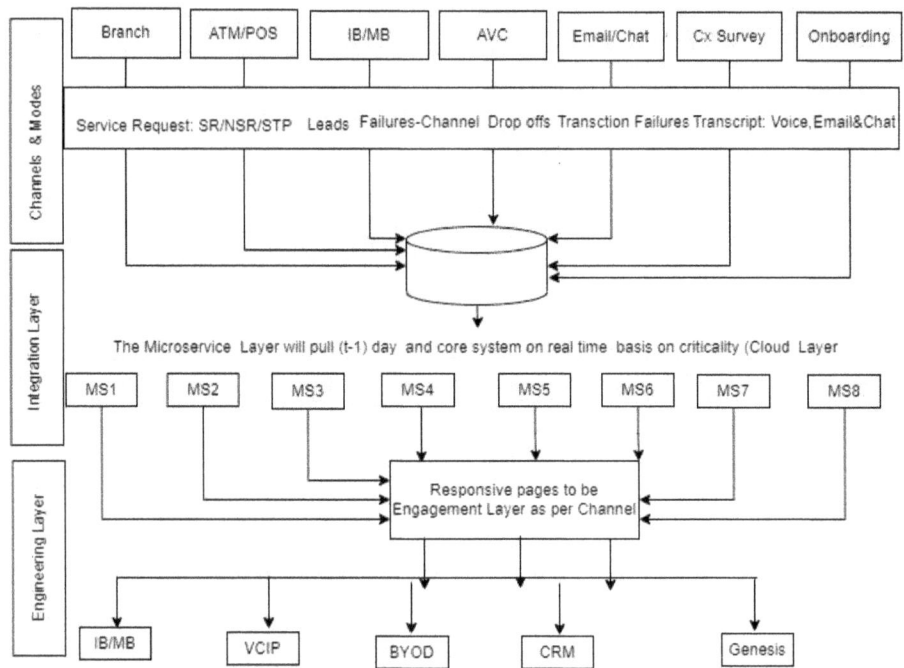

Fig 7.12: Centralized Platform of holding all data and Serving

Here is the target stage for improving the Customer's Credit Card Cheque experience:

1. The entire cycle used to take 8 days, but now it is being completed on the same day. The introduction of a Relationship Manager (RM) who deals with complicated cases.

2. We have established a comprehensive information and communication engine that triggers actions based on data points available in the Data Lake.

3. A Self-Service Portal will empower proactive customers to find solutions to their problems independently or with minimal guidance from the RM.

4. For customers facing more significant challenges, the RM can provide direct assistance through phone calls or SMS, following clear Standard Operating Procedures (SOP).

Customers can also receive basic training on using this self-help platform to manage their issues effectively."

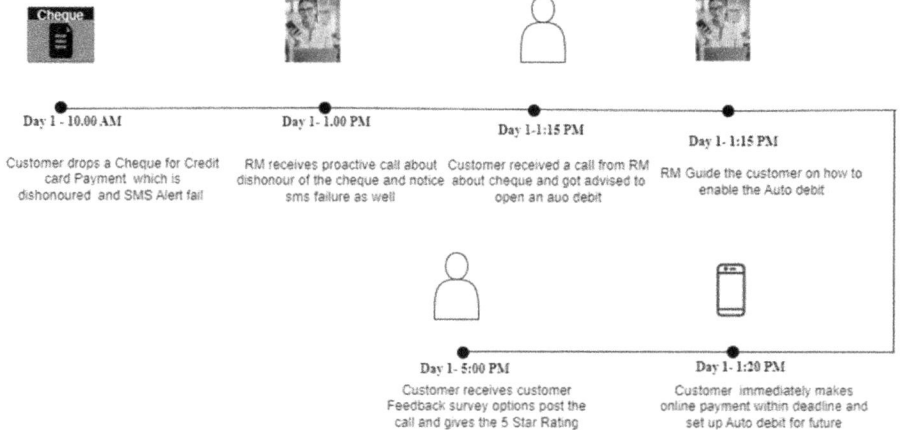

Fig 7.13: Same Day Customer complaint served

Chapter 8:
Digital Payment System

The rapid advancement of technology has given rise to a transformation in the way we conduct financial transactions. Digital payment systems have emerged as the cornerstone of this revolution, providing individuals, businesses, and economies with secure, convenient, and efficient ways to transfer money, make purchases, and manage finances. Digital payment systems facilitate the electronic transfer of funds between parties, eliminating the need for physical cash or checks. These systems offer various options such as mobile wallets, online banking, payment gateways, QR code payments, peer-to-peer transfers, and contactless payments. Robust security measures, including encryption and multi-factor authentication, ensure the safety of sensitive financial information during transactions.

The real time transactions of digital payment methods offer real-time processing, allowing transactions to occur instantaneously. These systems enable cross-border payments, making international transactions more accessible and cost-effective.

8.1 Benefits of Digital Payment Systems:

Digital payments offer the convenience of anytime, anywhere transactions, reducing the need to carry physical cash. Transactions occur quickly, facilitating rapid payments and reducing waiting times.

Digital payments often have lower transaction costs compared to traditional methods like checks and wire transfers. These systems provide digital records of transactions, simplifying financial tracking and budget management. It bridges the gap for individuals who lack access to traditional banking services, promoting financial inclusion. It contributes to economic growth by streamlining transactions and reducing friction in commerce. This drives economic efficiency by reducing the costs associated with handling physical cash, such as printing and transportation. A digital payment system encourages individuals to become more financially literate and tech-savvy. Advanced security features in digital payments help in reducing the risk of fraud compared to traditional methods.

The rise of digital payment systems has facilitated the growth of e-commerce, making online shopping more accessible and secure. Many governments encourage the adoption of digital payments to reduce the informal economy, enhance tax collection, and improve transparency. The reduction in the use of physical currency and checks contributes to environmental sustainability by decreasing paper usage.

The Need of Technology to deal with the challenge that Digital Payment is high. Cloud and AI plays the innovation role. Some of the challenges and future trends are Cybersecurity. Ensuring the security of digital payment systems remains a top concern due to the potential for cyber- attacks and data breaches.

Digital Divide While digital payments offer numerous benefits, the digital divide can hinder access for those without internet connectivity or smart phones. Often Regulation, striking a balance between innovation and regulatory oversight is essential to maintain consumer protection and financial stability.

Interoperability, As the number of digital payment systems grows, achieving interoperability between different platforms can be challenging and recently Contactless Technology speaks about Contactless payments, including NFC and QR codes, are becoming more prevalent, shaping the future of digital transactions.

8.2 Payment Vision

Need of High Tech, Cloud and AI to meet Payment Vision 2025 @ RBI, India

Integrity	Inclusion	Innovation	Institutionalization	Internationalization
-Weave in alternate authentication mechanism(s) from digital payment transactions -Borden scope, usage and relevance of Legal Entity Identifier(LEI) in all Payment activities -Expand interoperability to contactless transit card payments in offline mode -Enhance scalability and resilience of payment Systems -Leverage Online Dispute resolution(ODR) System for fraud monitoring and reporting	-Enable geo tagging of digital payment infrastructure and transactions -Revisit guidelines for prepaid payment instruments(PPIs) including closed system PPIs. -Consider Framework for regulation of all significant intermediaries in the payments ecosystem. -Bringing in enhancements to the Cheque Truncation System(CTS), including one nation, one grid clearing and settlement perspective. -Extend internal Ombudsman	- Facilitate framework for Internet of Things(IoT) and context based payments -Migrate all RBI operated payment system messages to ISO 20022 -Link credit cards and credit components of banking products to UPI -Create payment system for processing online merchant payments using internet/mobile banking -Organize payment innovation	-Comprehensive review of legislative aspects of the provisions and regulations of payment and settlement systems(PSS) Act -Constitute a payments advisory Council(PAC) to assist board for regulation and supervision of payment and settlement systems(BPSS) -Operationalize National card switch for card transactions at Point of Sale(PoS) and resultant settlements -Active Engagement and involvement in international fora(discussions of standard setting bodies)	-Global outreach of RTGS,NEFT,UPI And Rupay cards -Expand Structured Financial Messaging System(SFMS),Indian Financial Network(InFiNet) Frameworks across Jurisdictions. -Two Factor Authentication (2FA) for Cross-border card transactions. -Seek inclusion of INR in Continuous Linked Settlement(CLS) -Bring Further efficiencies in payment processing and settlements on introduction of central bank digital currencies(CBDSs) -Domestic and Cross-Border

-Provide enhancements to Central Payments Fraud information Registry(CPFIR) -Provide payee name look-up for fund transfers. -Increase proportionate oversight of payment -Include assessment of RTGS and NEFT under principles for financial market Infrastructures -Explore local processing of Payment transactions -Study creation of Digital payments protection fund(DPPF)	Scheme to all PSOs. -Support increase in market trading and settlement hours -Upscale customer outreach and awareness activities -Revisit scope and usefulness of payment Infrastructure development fund(PIDF) Scheme. -Attempt regulation of Big Techs and Fintech in payment space -Continue Endeavour to collect and publish granular, disaggregated payment systems data -Make payment systems more inclusive	contests and hackathons -Review needed for multiple payment identifiers. -Explore guidelines on payments involving buy now pay later(BNPL) Services		

8.3 Payment Cloud Architecture

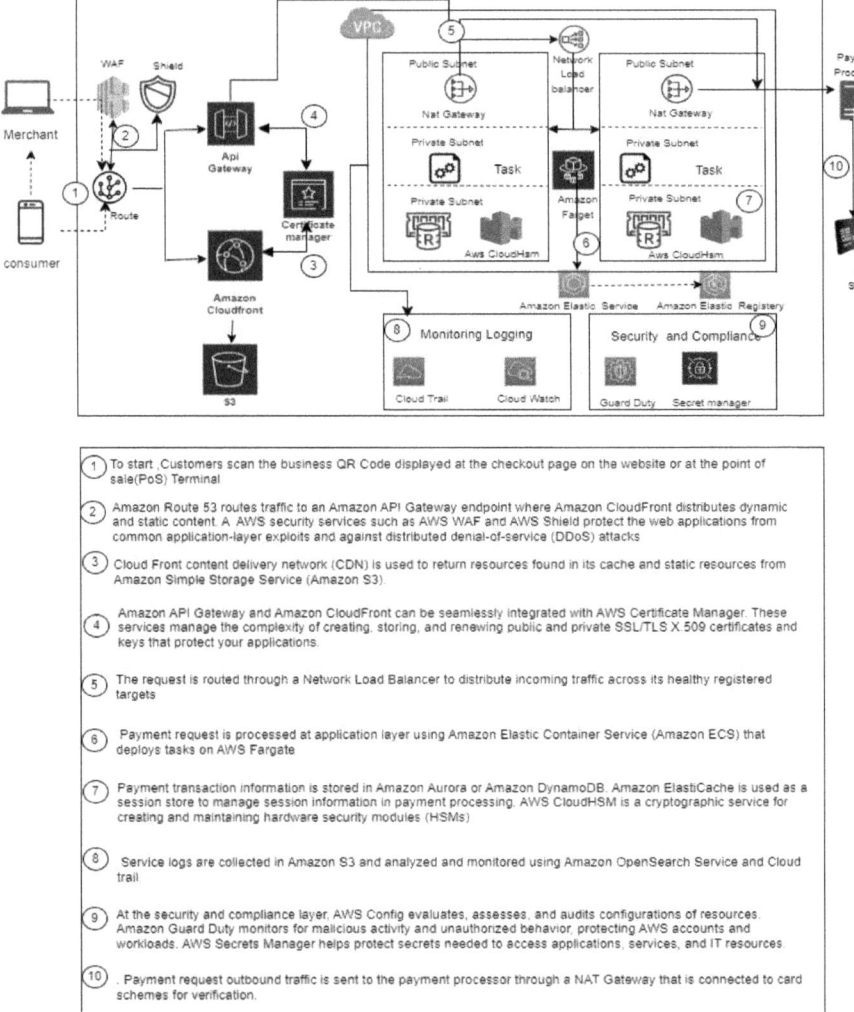

1. To start, Customers scan the business QR Code displayed at the checkout page on the website or at the point of sale(PoS) Terminal.

2. Amazon Route 53 routes traffic to an Amazon API Gateway endpoint where Amazon CloudFront distributes dynamic and static content. A AWS security services such as AWS WAF and AWS Shield protect the web applications from common application-layer exploits and against distributed denial-of-service (DDoS) attacks

3. Cloud Front content delivery network (CDN) is used to return resources found in its cache and static resources from Amazon Simple Storage Service (Amazon S3).

4. Amazon API Gateway and Amazon CloudFront can be seamlessly integrated with AWS Certificate Manager. These services manage the complexity of creating, storing, and renewing public and private SSL/TLS X.509 certificates and keys that protect your applications.

5. The request is routed through a Network Load Balancer to distribute incoming traffic across its healthy registered targets

6. Payment request is processed at application layer using Amazon Elastic Container Service (Amazon ECS) that deploys tasks on AWS Fargate

7. Payment transaction information is stored in Amazon Aurora or Amazon DynamoDB. Amazon ElastiCache is used as a session store to manage session information in payment processing. AWS CloudHSM is a cryptographic service for creating and maintaining hardware security modules (HSMs)

8. Service logs are collected in Amazon S3 and analyzed and monitored using Amazon OpenSearch Service and Cloud trail

9. At the security and compliance layer, AWS Config evaluates, assesses, and audits configurations of resources. Amazon Guard Duty monitors for malicious activity and unauthorized behavior, protecting AWS accounts and workloads. AWS Secrets Manager helps protect secrets needed to access applications, services, and IT resources.

10. Payment request outbound traffic is sent to the payment processor through a NAT Gateway that is connected to card schemes for verification.

Fig 8.1: Cloud Architecture for Payment Gateway with AWS

Chapter 9:
Data Lake – One of the Complex Use case of Cloud

DataLake -Good Problem to solve in Cloud

A data lake is a central repository that stores vast amounts of structured and unstructured data in its raw format, providing organizations with the flexibility to perform diverse analytics, data processing, and exploration tasks. When hosted in the cloud, data lakes offer a scalable and cost-effective solution for managing and analyzing large volumes of data. Here's an overview of data lakes in the cloud:

9.1 Strategy for Cloud Platform

A robust cloud strategy starts with a deep understanding of an organization's overarching goals and objectives. This involves assessing current challenges, identifying areas for improvement, and determining how cloud technology can address those needs. Whether the goal is to enhance operational efficiency, improve customer experience, or accelerate product development, a clear definition of business objectives helps shape the cloud strategy and align it with the organization's vision.

Choosing the right cloud model is a crucial decision that impacts the entire cloud strategy. Organizations can opt for public, private, hybrid, or multi-cloud models, depending on their specific requirements and considerations. Public clouds offer cost savings, scalability, and global accessibility, while private clouds provide enhanced security and control. Hybrid and multi-cloud approaches offer flexibility, enabling organizations to leverage the best features of multiple cloud environments. Selecting the appropriate cloud model involves evaluating factors such as data sensitivity, compliance requirements, performance needs, and cost considerations.

Four Dimensions – Strategy, Technology, Regulatory & Compliance, Risk & Security

- The process involves conducting discussions with key stakeholders and establishing a baseline for the current state of cloud adoption compared to the desired target state. It's essential to identify any gaps between the current and target states and then devise initiatives to bridge these gaps effectively.
- Furthermore, the evaluation of additional strategic choices, such as cloud maintenance strategies, exit strategies, and the target cloud operating model, is imperative. In parallel, various artifacts, including cloud adoption frameworks and cloud security checklists, must be developed to define the Bank's comprehensive cloud strategy and policy.
- The adoption of cloud technology is driven by several key business levers, including enhancing business capabilities and agility, establishing an appropriate organizational structure and operating model, fostering innovation through the consumption of external services, leveraging industry-specific solutions, optimizing workloads, and embracing a shared service model.

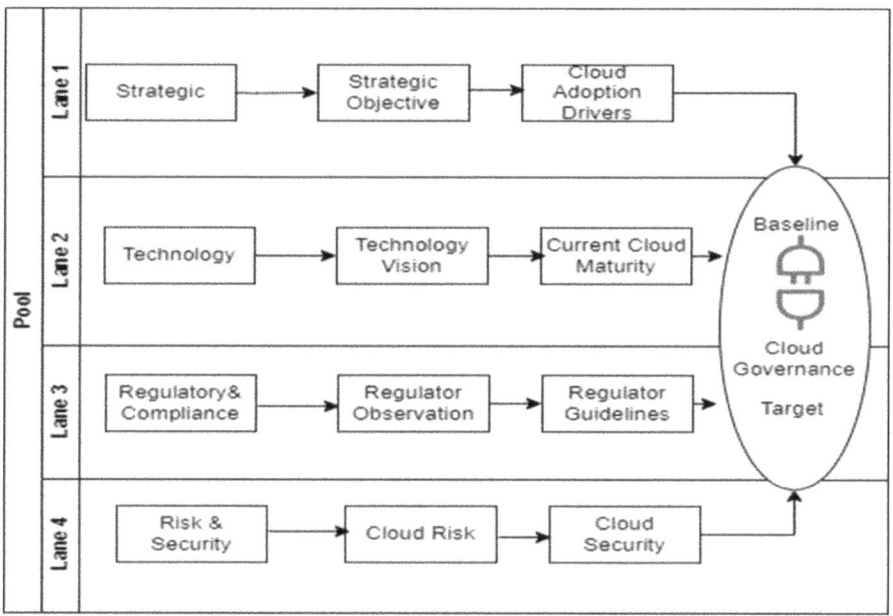

Fig 9.1: Strategy for Cloud Adoption

Why Multi cloud and Challenges :

- Avoiding Vendor Lock-In: By adopting a multi-cloud strategy, organizations can prevent reliance on a single cloud provider. This reduces the risk of being locked into a specific vendor's services, allowing for more flexibility and negotiation power in terms of pricing, features, and service-level agreements.
- Redundancy and Resilience: Multi-cloud architectures enable organizations to distribute workloads and data across multiple cloud providers. This redundancy helps mitigate the risk of service outages or disruptions. If one cloud provider experiences an issue, applications and data can seamlessly failover to another provider, ensuring continuity of operations.
- Performance Optimization: Different cloud providers may have varying strengths and capabilities in different areas. By adopting a multi-cloud approach, organizations can leverage specific cloud providers for their expertise in certain

technologies or regions, maximizing performance and ensuring the best user experience.
- Cost Optimization: Multi-cloud strategies allow organizations to optimize costs by selecting the most cost-effective services from different providers based on workload requirements. It provides the flexibility to choose between different pricing models, take advantage of spot instances or reserved instances, and avoid vendor-specific price hikes.
- Compliance and Data Sovereignty: Multi-cloud enables organizations to comply with regulatory requirements related to data sovereignty, privacy, and security. By leveraging cloud providers with data centers in specific regions, organizations can ensure compliance with local data protection laws and regulations.
- Innovation and Best-of-Breed Solutions: Different cloud providers offer unique services, APIs, and toolsets. Adopting a multi-cloud approach allows organizations to tap into the latest innovations and select the best-of-breed solutions from multiple providers, enabling faster time-to-market and driving competitive advantage.
- Disaster Recovery and Business Continuity: Multi-cloud architectures enhance disaster recovery capabilities by enabling organizations to replicate data and applications across multiple cloud providers. This ensures that in the event of a disaster or outage, business operations can be quickly restored from a different cloud provider.

There are several popular multi-cloud options available in the market today, including:
- Amazon Web Services (AWS): AWS is a comprehensive cloud computing platform provided by Amazon. It offers a wide range of services, including compute, storage, database,

networking, and AI, making it a popular choice for organizations looking for a robust multi-cloud solution.
- Microsoft Azure: Azure is a cloud computing service provided by Microsoft. It provides a vast array of services, including virtual machines, databases, analytics, and AI. Azure's strong integration with Microsoft's existing enterprise ecosystem makes it an attractive option for organizations using Microsoft technologies.
- Google Cloud Platform (GCP): GCP is a suite of cloud computing services provided by Google. It offers services such as computing, storage, machine learning, and data analytics. GCP's strength lies in its expertise in data analytics and AI, making it an appealing choice for organizations looking to leverage these capabilities.
- IBM Cloud: IBM Cloud is an enterprise-grade cloud computing platform that provides a range of services, including infrastructure, containers, AI, and blockchain. It focuses on offering robust security and compliance features, making it suitable for organizations with stringent regulatory requirements.
- Oracle Cloud: Oracle Cloud provides a comprehensive set of infrastructure and platform services, including compute, storage, networking, and database. It specializes in supporting enterprise workloads and offers strong integration with Oracle's on-premises software and applications.

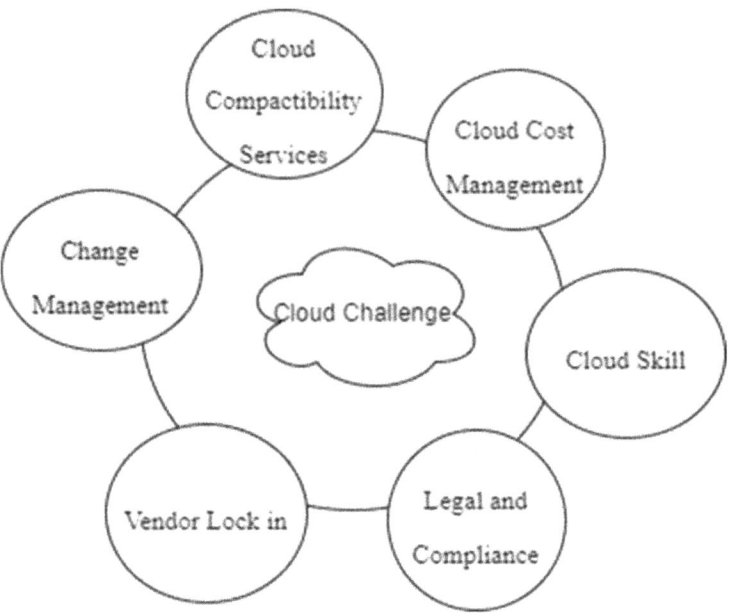

Cost is like un tapping water, Many measures have to be taken up
Expert Cloud skill resources are hard to find and built
Cross Border Data flow
Migration Complexity from On Prem to Cloud
Adoptive Resistance for Safe vs Unsafe

Fig 9.2: Cloud Challenge during Strategy

9.2 Build the Platform :

After defining the strategy and selecting a hyperscale, the next phase involves building the platform, a multifaceted endeavor that demands meticulous planning. Two critical aspects at the forefront of consideration are Infrastructure and Security.

Cloud Infrastructure and Security: Data lakes hosted in the cloud leverage the scalable and elastic nature of cloud infrastructure. A comprehensive cloud platform must address over 300 security controls, encompassing the creation of landing zones, activities related to control towers, architectural design, Virtual Private Clouds (VPCs), Virtual Networks (VNets), Express Routing, Cloud Hardware Security

Modules (HSMs) and Key Management Services (KMS), as well as Private HSM solutions like Gemalto. The selection of the appropriate Multiprotocol Label Switching (MPLS) and Express Route configurations for on-premises to cloud connectivity is a critical consideration.

Additionally, designing a North Star Architecture, defining Information Security (InfoSec) architectural requirements, and addressing open points are essential steps. Integration of various Security Information and Event Management (SIEM) solutions into the architecture must also be meticulously reviewed and implemented in conjunction with the bank's existing solutions.

Several Software Development Kits (SDKs) are available to facilitate key rotation and encryption. A key challenge is transporting Personally Identifiable Information (PII) and Sensitive Personal Data and Information (SPDI) to the cloud securely. To achieve this, data is encrypted during transit and at the persistence layer. During transit, data is wrapped in TLS 1.2 and transmitted via a dedicated MPLS connection to the cloud layer. Upon reaching the cloud, data is further encrypted using disk encryption. As an example, the process of CloudHSM and Key management in AWS is detailed. Similar concepts apply to other providers such as Azure, GCP, Oracle, and others.

AWS Key Management Services (KMS)

AWS KMS allows for your organization to create and control keys for cryptographic operations. This includes key generation, storage, management, and auditing when in the process of encrypting/decrypting or digitally signing data for applications or across AWS services. AWS KMS allows the ability of complete security through managed encryption keys across AWS platforms.

Centralized key management gives the user a central point of control for managing keys and defining access policies throughout all integrated AWS services. With AWS KMS, you will have the ability to create a customer master key (CMK) generally known as a master key, use a master key, create and export a data key encrypted by a master key, enable/disable master keys, and audit the usage of master keys in AWS CloudTrail.

AWS incorporates Master keys and Data keys. The Master key will not leave the AWS KMS service in an unencrypted form. With AWS KMS, specific access policies can be set for only trusted users that can use CMKs. In AWS KMS, Bring your own key (BYOK) feature is available to import your own key material into that CMK, however, the imported key material is supported only for symmetric CMKs in AES-256-XTS keys in PKCS#1 standard format. AWS KMS can be paired with AWS CloudHSM cluster to create the key material for a CMK that can be managed by AWS KMS service.

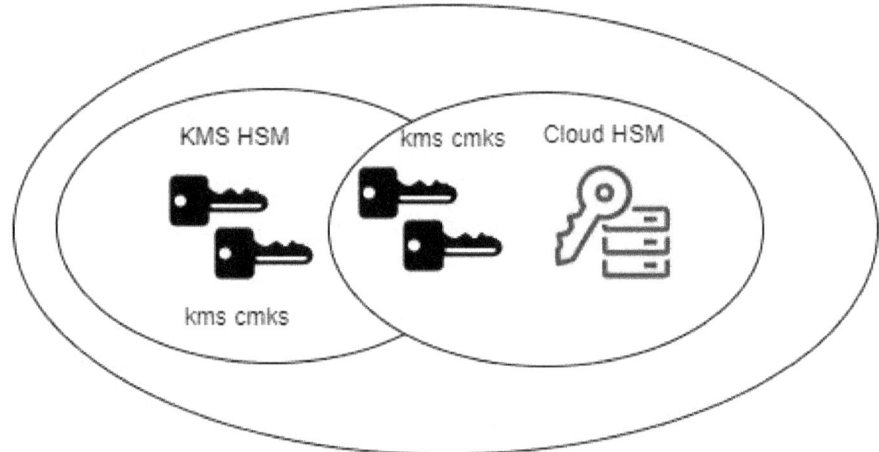

Fig 9.3: CloudHSM with Key Vault

AWS CloudHSM :

Many regulators require banks to utilize dedicated encryption keys rather than shared ones. Banks often opt for solutions like Gemalto, which enables them to use their dedicated encryption keys on their premises or employ a dedicated Key Vault provided by the cloud provider. In this instance, I will elaborate on the use of a cloud provider's dedicated Cloud Hardware Security Module (HSM).

AWS CloudHSM is a cloud-based hardware security module that is owned and managed by the customer. It operates as a single-tenant hardware module, ensuring that it is not shared with other customers or applications. Organizations can leverage AWS CloudHSM to harness the capabilities of HSMs for encryption key management without the complexities of managing HSM hardware in their own data centers.

AWS CloudHSM enables the creation of FIPS 140-2 Level 3 overall validated single-tenant HSM clusters within an Amazon Virtual Private Cloud (VPC), providing a secure environment for storing and utilizing encryption keys. Users have complete control over how these keys are used, facilitated by a separate authentication mechanism distinct from AWS credentials.

AWS CloudHSM serves various use cases, including the management of Public/Private key pairs for Public Key Infrastructure (PKI), code and document signing, secure storage of private keys for services such as databases, storage systems, and web applications, as well as key storage for Digital Rights Management (DRM) solutions.

By incorporating AWS CloudHSM, organizations can align with key management compliance requirements while benefiting from Hardware Security Modules overseen by AWS and the ability to integrate multiple platforms for secure key storage.

9.3 Design Consideration :

Please note that when employing a custom key store, you are essentially creating a 'kms user' CU (customer) account within your AWS CloudHSM cluster. Subsequently, you provide the credentials for the 'kms user' account to AWS Key Management Service (KMS).

This approach necessitates that your service provider is capable of using KMS as the key management solution within their application. Given that SaaS providers cannot directly interact with the CloudHSM cluster, they must rely on KMS APIs to encrypt data. If your SaaS provider performs encryption within their application without utilizing KMS, this option may not be suitable for your needs.

When implementing a custom key store, it's crucial not only to manage access to the CloudHSM cluster but also to oversee access to AWS KMS. Since both the custom key store and KMS reside within your account, you must grant the SaaS provider permission to utilize specific KMS keys. This can be achieved by enabling cross-account access. For detailed guidance on this process, please refer to the blog post titled 'Share custom encryption keys more securely between accounts by using AWS Key Management Service.'

For streamlined setup,

I recommend dedicating a separate AWS account specifically for the Cloud HSM cluster and custom key store, as this simplifies the overall configuration.

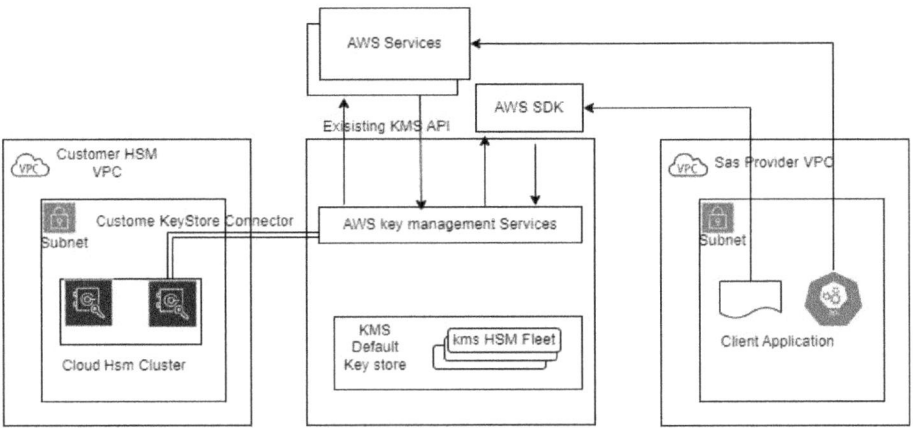

Fig 9.4: A Cluster HSM instance is connected to KMS to create a Customer controlled Key store

2. Preparing for DataLake

In the realm of Data Lakes, the concept of 'defense' encompasses measures taken to safeguard and secure data, while 'offense' refers to the strategies employed to extract value and insights from the stored data.

In the context of Defense: I speak about

Data Security: This involves the implementation of robust security measures, including encryption, access controls, and authentication, to thwart unauthorized access to sensitive data residing in the Data Lake.

Data Privacy: Ensuring compliance with data privacy regulations by employing techniques such as anonymization or pseudonymization of personal information. Additionally, mechanisms are established to manage consent effectively.

Data Governance: Establishing policies and processes for data quality, metadata management, data lineage, and data retention to uphold the integrity of the stored data.

Threat Detection and Prevention: Employing intrusion detection systems, firewalls, and security analytics to identify and preempt cyber threats and attacks targeting the Data Lake.

Auditing and Monitoring: Implementation of continuous monitoring and auditing mechanisms to track user activities, data access, and changes, fostering transparency and accountability.

Access Controls: Utilizing role-based access controls (RBAC) and fine-grained permissions to ensure that only authorized individuals can access specific data within the Data Lake.

In terms of Offense: I speak about

Data Analysis: Leveraging advanced analytics tools to extract valuable insights, discern patterns, and identify trends within the diverse datasets residing in the Data Lake, thereby facilitating data-driven decision-making.

Machine Learning and AI: The application of machine learning and artificial intelligence techniques to develop predictive models, recommendations, and automation based on the extensive data available in the Data Lake.

Real-time Analytics: The utilization of real-time data streaming and processing technologies to conduct immediate analytics, enabling prompt insights into evolving data patterns.

Cross-functional Collaboration: Encouraging collaboration between different departments and teams to share insights and explore data from multiple perspectives, fostering innovation and well-informed decision-making.

Data Exploration & Monetization: Empowering data scientists and analysts to delve into raw and unstructured data within the Data Lake to unearth hidden patterns and insights. This approach enables the extraction of additional value by providing data-driven services, insights, or datasets to external partners, customers, or stakeholders.

Customer Insights: Analyzing customer data from various Data Lake sources to gain a deep understanding of customer behaviors, preferences, and needs, ultimately enhancing the customer experience.

Business Intelligence: Leveraging the Data Lake to support business intelligence endeavors, including the creation of dashboards, reporting, and visualizations, to enhance strategic planning and performance monitoring.

9.4 Functional View of DataLake

Prior to crafting the DataLake architecture, it is imperative to explore the diverse functional perspectives where the Data Landscape is distributed across various segments. This approach empowers organizations to engage in advanced analytics, unearth valuable insights, and uncover patterns that may have remained elusive when employing conventional data storage methodologies. Data scientists and analysts can conduct comprehensive data exploration spanning various sources to attain a deeper understanding and facilitate well-informed decision-making. The diagram below provides an overview of the Data opportunities within six major areas.

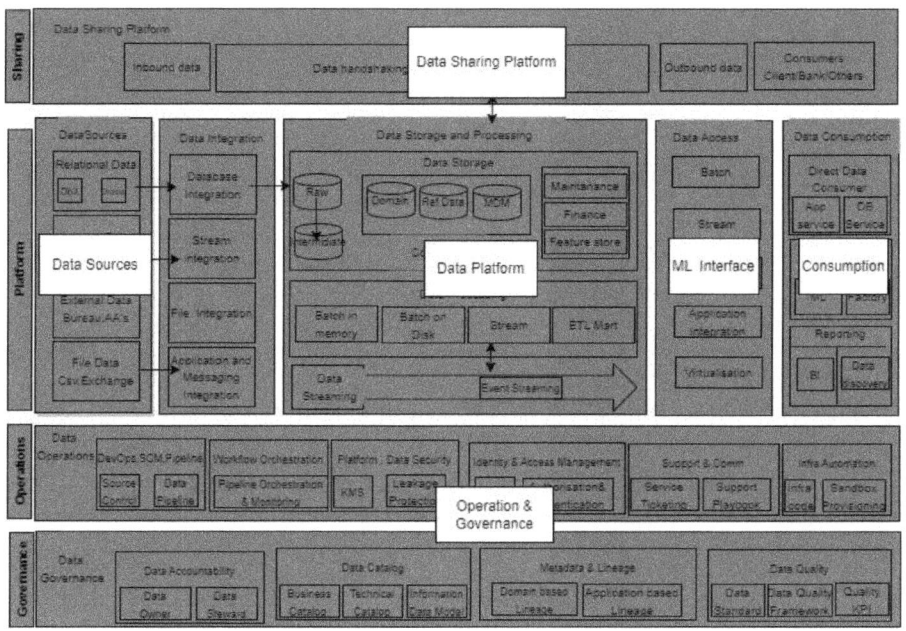

Fig 9.5: Grid for Data Opportunities and Focus

9.5 DataLake Architecture :

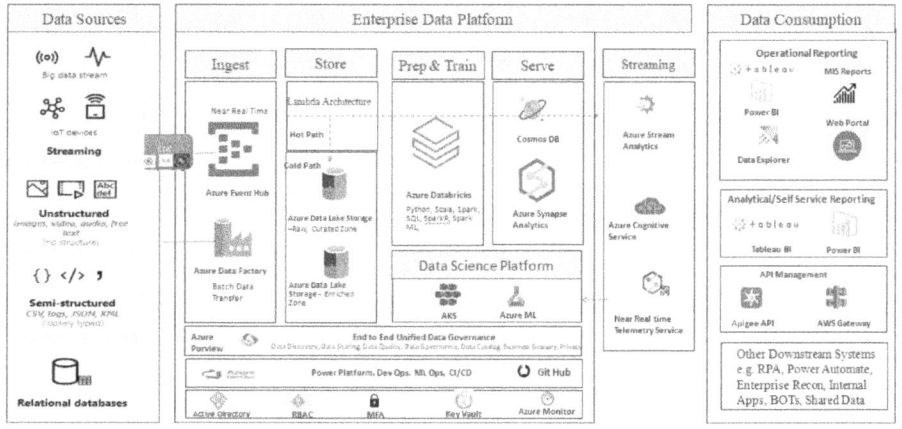

Fig 9.6: One of DataLake Architecture in Azure

Data Ingestion: Data lakes support the ingestion of various types of data, including structured, semi-structured, and unstructured data from sources like databases, logs, IoT devices, and external APIs. Cloud data lakes enable batch processing as well as real-time streaming of data. With the ability to ingest petabytes of data with auto-evolving schemas, data engineers can deliver fast, reliable, scalable and automatic data for analytics, data science or machine learning. Most of FI/Bank has Core Product Processor Data, CASA, Loan, Credit Card, Wholesale/Corporate Data, SMB, Payment, Channels like IB/MB etc, DLP(Digital Landing Platform) data , Bureau data, Social data, Investment bank's data, Fixed income product, Hedge fund ,Commercial Product data etc has to be ingested to DataLake for various Analytics and Regulatory purpose.

In the architecture depicted above, the influx of streaming data into the DataLake is facilitated through streaming technologies such as Kafka and real-time Change Data Capture (CDC) solutions like GoldenGate (GG), IBM CDC, Attunity, and Informatica CDC, among others. To enable the 'Hot Path,' Azure Event Hub plays a pivotal role. The real-time ingestion framework operates dynamically, accommodating schema evolution while relying on offsets.

A range of control mechanisms are implemented to ensure data governance and oversee the validation of datasets, among other aspects

Streaming Scenario for Ingestion:

Use Azure Event Hubs or Azure IoT Hubs to take the data streaming data client applications or IoT devices by use of the above approach. Event Hubs or IoT Hub will then store streaming data preserving the sequence of events received. Consumers can then connect to Event Hubs or IoT Hub endpoints and retrieve messages for processing.

Store

Within the Raw data lake layer, organize your data lake following the best practices around which layers to create, what folder structures to use in each layer and what files format to use for each analytics scenario.

Configure Event Hubs Capture or IoT Hub Storage Endpoints to save a copy of the events into the Raw layer of your Azure Data Lake Store Gen 2 data lake. This feature implements the "Cold Path" of the Lambda architecture pattern and allows you to perform historical and trend analysis on the stream data saved in your data lake using SQL Serverless queries or Spark notebooks following the pattern for semi-structured data sources described above.

Prep and Train:

For real-time insights, use a Stream Analytics job to implement the "Hot Path" of the Lambda architecture pattern and derive insights from the stream data in transit. Define at least one input for the data stream coming from your Event Hubs or IoT Hub, one query to process the input data stream and one Power BI output to where the query results will be sent to.

As part of your data processing with Stream Analytics, you can invoke machine-learning models to enrich your stream datasets and drive business decisions based on the predictions generated. These machine-learning models can be consumed from Azure Cognitive Services or from custom ML models in Azure Machine learning.

Use other Stream Analytics job outputs to send processed events to Azure Synapse SQL pools or Data Explorer pools for further analytics use cases.

For near real-time telemetry and time-series analytics scenarios, use Data Explorer pools to easily ingest IoT events directly from Event Hubs or IoT Hubs. With Data Explorer pools, you can use Kusto queries (KQL) to perform time-series analysis, geospatial clustering, and machine learning enrichment.

Serve

Business analysts then use Power BI real-time datasets and dashboard capabilities to visualize the fast changing insights generated by your Stream Analytics query.

Data can also be securely shared to other business units or external trusted partners using Azure Data Share. Data consumers have the freedom to choose what data format they want to use and also what compute engine is best to process the shared datasets.

Batching Scenario of Ingestion (Structure, Unstructured of Core Product Processor Data)

The Ingestion Framework for Batching is most sophisticated and carries many scenarios and follow the guiding principle of DataLake

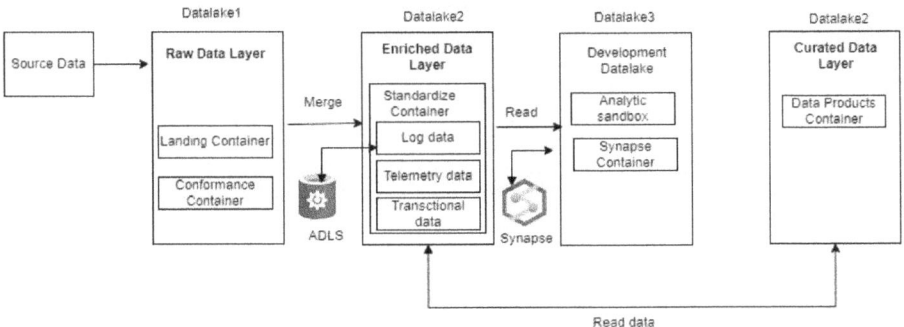

Fig 9.7: Different Layer during Ingestion and Storing Process

Raw layer :

Think of the raw layer as a reservoir that stores data in its natural and original state. It's unfiltered and unpurified. You might store the data in its original format, such as JSON or CSV. Or it might be cost effective to store the file contents as a column in a compressed file format, like Avro, Parquet, or Databricks Delta Lake.

This raw data is immutable. Keep your raw data locked down, and if you give permissions to any consumers, automated or human, ensure that they're read-only. You can organize this layer by using one folder per source system. Give each ingestion process write access to only its associated folder. When you load data from source systems into the raw zone, you can choose to do:

- **Full loads** to extract a full data set.

- **Delta loads** to load only changed data.

Indicate your chosen loading pattern in your folder structure to simplify use for your data consumers. Raw data from source systems for each source-aligned data application or automated ingestion engine source lands in the full folder or the delta folder. Each ingestion process should have written access to only its associated folder.

The differences between full loads and delta loads are:

- **Full load** - Complete data from the source can be on boarded if:
    - The data volume at the source is small.
    - The source system doesn't maintain a timestamp field that identifies if data has been added, updated, or deleted.
    - The source system overwrites the complete data each time.
- **Delta load** - Incremental data from the source can be on boarded if:
    - The data volume at the source is large.
    - The source system maintains a timestamp field that identifies if data has been added, updated, or deleted.
    - The source system creates and updates files on data changes.

Your raw data lake is composed of your landing and conformance containers. Each container uses a 100% mandatory folder structure specific to its purpose.

Enriched layer :

Think of the enriched layer as a filtration layer. It removes impurities and can also involve enrichment.

Your standardization container holds systems of record and masters. Folders are segmented first by subject area, then by entity. Data is available in merged, partitioned tables that are optimized for analytics consumption. This data layer is considered the silver layer or read data source. Data within this layer has had no transformations applied other than data quality, delta lake conversion, and data type alignment.

Curated layer :

Your curated layer is your consumption layer. It's optimized for analytics rather than data ingestion or processing. The curated layer might store data in denormalized data marts or star schemas. Data from your standardized container is transformed into high-value data products that are served to your data consumers. This data has structure. It can be served to the consumers as-is, such as data science notebooks, or through another read data store, such as Azure SQL Database.

Use tools, like Spark or Data Factory, to do dimensional modeling instead of doing it inside your database engine. This use of tools becomes a key point if you want to make your lake the single source of truth. If you do dimensional modeling outside of your lake, you might want to publish models back to your lake for consistency. This layer isn't a replacement for a data warehouse. Its performance typically isn't adequate for responsive dashboards or end user and consumer interactive analytics.

This layer is best suited for internal analysts and data scientists who run large-scale, improvised queries or analysis, or for advanced analysts who don't have time-sensitive reporting needs. Because storage costs are lower in your data lake than your data warehouse, it can be cost effective to keep granular, low-level data in your lake. Store aggregated data in your warehouse. Generate these aggregations by using Spark or Azure Data Factory. Persist them to your data lake before loading them into your data warehouse.

Data assets in this zone are typically highly governed and well documented. Assign permissions by department or by function, and organize permissions by consumer group or data mart.

During these three layers of Data pipeline Observability capabilities include A high-quality, high-fidelity lineage diagram that provides visibility into how data flows for impact analysis, Granular logging with performance and status of the data pipeline at a row level, Continuous monitoring of data pipeline jobs to ensure continued operation

Improve data reliability throughout the data lake house so data teams can confidently trust the information for downstream initiatives by: Defining data quality and integrity controls within the pipeline with defined data expectations, Addressing data quality errors with predefined policies (fail, drop, alert, quarantine) , Leveraging the data quality metrics that are captured, tracked and reported for the entire data pipeline

Data Cataloging and Management: Cloud data lakes provide tools for cataloging and managing data. Metadata, tags, and data lineage information can be associated with stored data to facilitate discovery and governance.

Schema on Read: One of the key features of data lakes is the "schema on read" approach. Data is stored in its raw format, and the schema is applied when the data is read for analysis. This allows for flexibility in data exploration and analysis without the need to structure the data upfront.

Chapter 10: The open banking transformation:

With the arrival of the digital revolution, sharing of data has become easier as well as necessary. This requires the data generated to be apportioned to all who might need it for various purposes. This is where fintech (an amalgamation of the terms finance and technology) firms come in. The data generated by Financial Institutions including banks are shared with fintech firms through the means of application programming interface (APIs), which acts as the bridge between the two entities. Thus, APIs facilitate data sharing in the banking sector, which brings about the concept of open banking. This has led to FIs offering consumer-centric and personalized services.

Open Banking can be defined as a mechanism where data is shared freely with the consent of the consumer, in order to generate the required analytics and provide financial and other services. Since consent is an essential ingredient of the concept of open banking, it is popularly regarded that open banking promotes the customers' control over the data they generate.

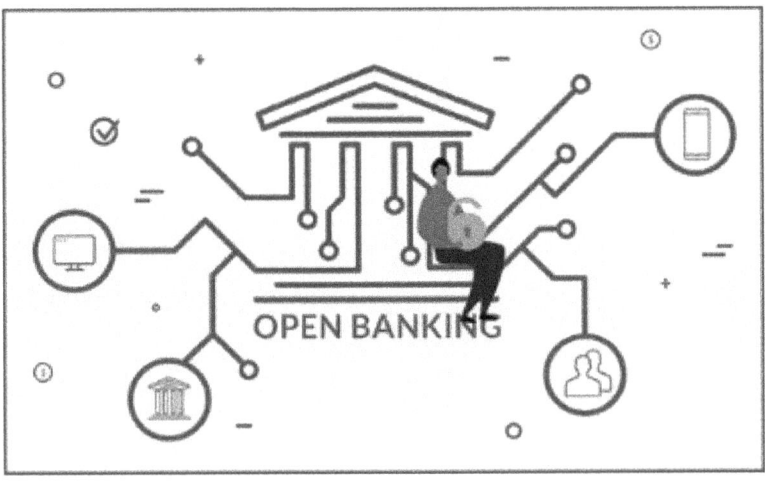

> Since the awareness regarding the sanctity of one's data is gaining salience, this, so to say, 'advantage' of open banking is what makes it prominent among both banks and consumers alike. The essential principle of user consent is embodied in the Information Technology Act, 2000 as well as the forthcoming Personal Data Protection Bill, 2019.

10.1 The Indian Model

In 2016, Account Aggregators (or 'AAs') were developed by the Reserve Bank of India through a Master Direction to facilitate the open banking regime. Ordinarily, the data was shared between the providers and the users of information (for the sake of simplicity, otherwise known as FIPs and FIUs, respectively) directly, which rendered the process opaque and deprived customer control. Being impartial third-party operators, AAs are based on a strict consensual model, operating on authorization agreements between the customer, the bank, and themselves. They are merely channels through which data will pass based on consent and are not allowed to access, store, or utilize the data handled by them. The directions also provide for an IT framework including the consent architecture and operational mechanism for the AAs.

Think of the AAs as a broker for customers' financial information. Once the customer grants consent that their *specific data* may be shared with *particular FIs seeking it* (FIUs) for the *mentioned purpose* for a *certain period*, the AAs procure the same from the FI holding the data (by virtue of them serving the customer, the FIPs) and deliver it to the FIUs. On the basis of the data so received the latter may offer new financial services to the consumer. Meanwhile, the AAs are regulated by the RBI and its directions. The customers also have the option of revoking their consent in respect of the time period, the FIU, and the particular data shared.

The Master Direction also specifies that an AA may be registered as an NBFC, granting the RBI the power to govern them, and also be registered with a bank. Further, a company performing the function of an AA may not carry any other business. As of yet, seven AAs have been granted approval to operate as AAs, three of which have only an in-principle approval. The framework went live recently, on September 2, 2021, with prominent banks joining in.

To address concerns relating to the functioning of the three different kinds of entities and difficulties that may arise in coordination, the DigiSahamati Foundation was established as a member collective. The organization works towards ensuring that the members adhere to the technical standards as well as to manage the competing interests.

What makes the Indian approach different is that the intermediary, or the AA, is directly regulated under the Directions of the RBI. The model is very similar to that in the UK where the regime of open banking is government-regulated through the Open Banking Standard, as a part of the Open Banking Implementation Entity, wherein a data sharing or API framework is prescribed and enforced by independent parties, to tackle the competitive concerns.

10.2 Concern in the Open Banking:

Even though data sharing is the widely accepted way forward, expected to overhaul the financial and other related sectors, the concept is only in its nascent stage, having been operationalized by the European Union in 2018. Issues of security and privacy are rife in the emerging field of open banking. The concerns have been predicted and provided for, to some extent, in the RBI Directives through the measures for Data Security, granting customer rights including a record of consent and disability of the AA to use the data for any purpose other than that authorized by them, as well as the requirement of a grievance redressal mechanism for the customers.

However, considering that AAs would also be large companies, working closely with FIPs and FIUs, the possibility of abuse of market power, as well as imbalance of power with respect to the data principal or the user, cannot be completely disregarded. There is also the issue of low digital literacy and lack of access to smartphones, especially among the poor. As is the case with every digitization move, AAs also fall under the bridging or deepening the 'digital divide' debate. Further, click consent, though a quick and easy way to achieve the mandate of open banking, may leave customers vulnerable to misuse of data as they may not understand where or how their information is being used.

While we talked about the Indian model, similar below is the western European and USA and the rise of open banking enables FIs to provide a better customer experience via data sharing between consumers, the concept Global bank believes in FIs and third-party service providers through APIs. An example of this is Payment Services Directive (PSD2), which transformed financial services in the EU region as part of Open Banking Europe regulation. As a result, FIs have access to more data from multiple banks and service providers, including customer account and transaction data. This trend has expanded within the world of fraud and financial crimes with the latest guidance from FinCEN under section 314(b) of USA Patriot Act; covered FIs can now share information with other FIs and within domestic and foreign branches regarding individuals, entities, organizations and so on that are suspected to be involved in potential money laundering.

While information sharing provision helps with transparency and protects the United States financial systems against money laundering and terrorism financing, the information exchange must be done using protocols with proper data and security protections. To solve the problem of securing information sharing, Databricks recently announced Delta Sharing, an open and secure protocol for data sharing. Using familiar open source APIs, such as pandas and Spark, data producers and consumers can now share data using secure and open protocols and maintain a full audit of all the data transactions to maintain compliance with FinCEN regulations

10.3 Architecture - Open Banking

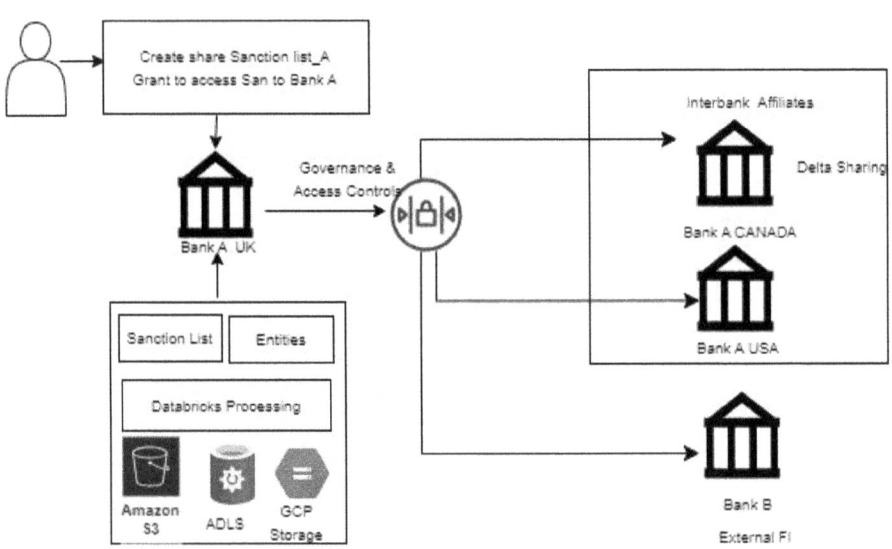

Fig 10.1: Open Banking Architecture

Chapter 11:
HSBC Creation of AQM using GCP

Financial institutions worldwide are selecting Google Cloud Platform to modernize their operations, enhance operational resilience, and excel in the digital, post-pandemic economy. Several compelling reasons support this choice.

11.1 Modernizing data warehousing and scaling intelligent analytics

Increasing data volume often results in untapped potential due to traditional data warehouse complexities. Typically, 85% of time is spent on system engineering tasks, leaving only 15% for data analysis. Moreover, scalability issues persist.

Google's BigQuery, a serverless, scalable data warehousing solution, automates system engineering tasks, providing a simplified interface. It eliminates upfront hardware provisioning and scales automatically for optimal query performance. Complex queries benefit from distributed computing across multiple servers. With vast resources, BigQuery can swiftly analyze petabyte-sized datasets. Migration to BigQuery can reduce total ownership costs by 41% to 52%.

11.2 Assistance for hybrid and multi-cloud setups.

Google's global-scale infrastructure ensures security and control. While a major hardware manufacturer, Google exclusively uses its servers internally. GCP encrypts data in transit and at rest by default. Developers can apply application-layer encryption for maximum data security. Google Cloud only accesses customer data when necessary for contractual obligations, with strict access controls enforced. Regular audits verify compliance.

11.3 Robust yet user-friendly AI and machine learning tools.

Google Cloud provides a range of AI and machine learning tools for developers, analysts, and non-data science professionals. For instance, BigQuery ML lets data analysts create and deploy custom ML models using basic SQL. These models can be refined using Google's public datasets, covering topics like weather and COVID-19 tracking. LendingDoc AI, part of Google Cloud's Document AI tools, is tailored for the mortgage industry. It automates mortgage document reviews, reducing processing time, enhancing data capture, and ensuring regulatory compliance. This benefits both borrowers and lenders.

11.4 Mission Critical Services

In finance, even a single minute of downtime can result in millions of dollars in lost revenue, and any incident can have serious consequences. To meet the demands of such critical environments, Google Cloud offers Mission Critical Services (MCS), an exclusive consultative service for GCP Premium Support customers. MCS goes beyond premium support, partnering closely with customers on their cloud journey. It leverages proven methodologies developed by Google's Site Reliability Engineering (SRE) teams over two decades, which Google Cloud also uses for its own infrastructure.Google's top-tier engineers, deeply familiar with MCS customers' workloads, provide around-the-clock monitoring, prevention, and incident resolution. Unlike Google's Premium Support with a 15-minute response time, MCS customers enjoy a rapid five-minute response. A dedicated team rapidly diagnoses and resolves issues within this timeframe.

11.5 Case Study

HSBC, a digital banking leader, conducts more than 90% of its global and Hong Kong retail transactions via digital platforms. Nevertheless, amidst the rising popularity of digital banking, call centers remain a crucial channel for the bank.

Customers value the "human touch" offered by call center services, particularly when they require assistance. However, efficiently managing high call volumes, especially in a market like Hong Kong, where many individuals speak a blend of Cantonese and English, often with literal translations, poses a significant challenge. Handling such speech styles demands considerable experience. Ensuring quality in this context typically involves a labor-intensive and manual process.

Addressing this challenge presented HSBC's contact center teams with a particularly complex AI problem. Compounded by the absence of existing open-source data or machine learning models, it demanded innovative solutions. Collaborating with Google Cloud, the bank has implemented automation for quality assessments of its contact center sales calls, resulting in substantial time savings and enhanced customer experiences. This achievement was realized through the creation of a Natural Language Processing (NLP) solution tailored for reviewing conversations in Cantonese-English at the contact center.

The bank's Intelligence Hub constitutes a dedicated team of data scientists, engineers, and architects committed to the migration of HSBC's data and analytics workflows onto Google Cloud. Their primary objective is to harness the potential of data through AI and machine learning. This specialized team collaborates closely with various departments and business units within the bank to conceive and construct comprehensive data and AI solutions. To achieve this, they employed Google Cloud APIs such as AutoML Natural Language and speech-to-text to train machine language models, enabling the classification, extraction, and detection of customer sentiment. By harnessing Google Cloud computing resources and utilizing BigQuery as a data analytics warehouse, they implemented Google's AI-driven Speech-to-Text technology to accurately transcribe spoken combinations of Cantonese and English.

The outcome of this endeavor was the development of an Automatic Quality Management system (AQM), a pioneering in-house voice-processing solution empowered by AI. The AQM plays a pivotal role in identifying areas of improvement in customer conversations, marking a significant milestone for HSBC's Hong Kong Call Centre. The solution aids in promptly pinpointing sales agents in need of coaching and enhancement. Automated alerts notify the monitoring team about these calls, facilitating timely agent support. Moreover, the bank gains additional insights to refine its customer service, which prove valuable for designing future customer experiences and staff training. This eliminates the need for dedicating 1,200 man-hours to monitor 100% of sales calls, significantly reducing monitoring time.

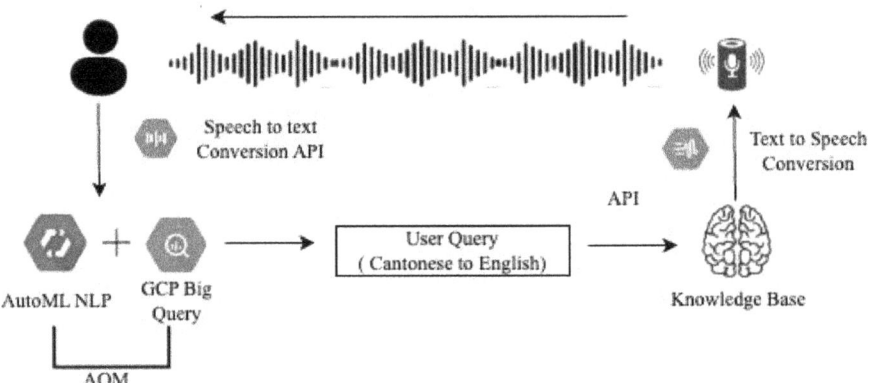

Fig 11.1: GCP Speech to Text Solution

Chapter 12 :
Data Migration from on Prem to Cloud :The Fundamentals

Cloud migration is the movement of data, applications, and other IT services into the cloud. In this piece, we're mainly discussing on-premises to cloud migration — i.e., the transfer of the data hosted in your in-house data center and other infrastructure to an infrastructure-as-a-service (IaaS) or platform-as-a-service (PaaS) cloud deployment.

12.1 The 4 types of cloud migration for Application :

Rehosting: Also, commonly known as the "lift-and-shift" or "forklift migration" approach, rehosting is the simplest type of on-premises to cloud migration. Applications, data, schema, and workloads are moved from the data center to an IaaS cloud deployment, without being changed in any way. While this type of migration is fairly easy to accomplish, it limits what you can do with your apps because they haven't been modified to be cloud-native. It's best suited for select low-impact, on-premises workloads, or as the initial migration method for organizations new to the cloud.

Refactoring: This strategy, sometimes called "rip and replace" or "redesign," is much more labor- and time-intensive than rehosting. It entails rewriting and restructuring the architecture of apps — and, potentially, data and schemas — either before or after migration; post-migration is more common. The key benefit of refactoring is that you essentially redesign apps from the ground up with the cloud in mind, taking advantage of the latest, most advanced features your cloud service provider (CSP) has to offer. Initial cloud migration costs may be higher, but in the long run, your cloud tools will run more effectively. If you intend to move a lot of your apps and workloads off-premises, refactoring may ultimately be the best choice.

Replatforming: Falling somewhere between rehosting and refactoring, replatforming involves making some changes to an application while keeping some of its other core elements. Because of this, it's sometimes referred to as "move and improve," or "revise." A common example would be modifying the way in which an app interacts with the database. Replatforming can work for migrations from on-premises infrastructure to IaaS, as well as moves to a PaaS service.

Replacing: In this migration strategy, data is taken from existing on-premises applications and moved to cloud-based software-as-a-service (SaaS) apps created by third parties, while the original in-house apps are discarded. This approach may make sense for enterprises that have had their apps compromised in some way or are simply working with legacy tools that they consider inferior to third-party SaaS options.

12.2 The 2 types of Cloud Migration for Data :

What is offline cloud migration?

In an offline migration, an enterprise uses physical storage media -- such as portable disk drives or storage appliances -- to move workloads to a cloud environment. Under this method, admins acquire portable storage media, copy data from local systems onto it, then physically deliver the media to a cloud provider. After that, the provider uploads the data to its cloud via a local network connection -- which is faster than the public internet or connects the storage media directly to its cloud servers. Once data is in the cloud, the offline migration is considered complete and the portable storage media can be decommissioned or reused.

This on-premises-to-cloud migration approach usually costs more than an online transfer because enterprises need to rent or purchase large volumes of storage media, and then pay to relocate it. This method also typically requires more planning and effort than an online migration because admins must acquire portable storage media and manage the multistep process of moving it physically to a cloud provider. They must also manage the physical security risks that could arise from unauthorized parties accessing portable storage media that contains sensitive data. Most of the below cloud providers provide a separate physical box where data can be encrypted using SHA 256, Separate key and vault . The vehicle transfers it without a tracking mechanism on where the Vehicle. Once Physical data got connected to the server, then only it got to know. However, it is a bit concerning for Infosec front to get this approval which is very valid because of PII and SPDI DataSet.

Offline migrations can also be performed using cloud vendors' own services or third-party tools. Popular options are: AWS Snowball, AWS Snowmobile, Google Data Transfer Appliance, Azure Data Box, IBM Cloud Mass, Data Migration, RiverMeadow

What is online cloud migration?

An online cloud migration uses a network -- either a cloud provider's direct connection service or the public internet -- to transfer data and applications to a cloud data center in real time. Online migrations are simpler overall because IT teams can copy data in one step from their local infrastructure to the cloud. Online migration typically also offers cost savings compared to offline approaches, because the only expense is whatever it costs to pay for the bandwidth necessary to transfer data from on premises to a cloud. Most cloud providers don't charge ingress fees for incoming data -- they only charge for egress, meaning data that leaves their clouds -- so there's no added cost due to ingress.

For example, if an organization has only 1 TB of data to migrate and a 1 GBps network connection is available, the online migration should take under three hours using a standard internet connection. However, 1,000 TB would likely take more than 100 days to transfer over the same network connection in which case, an offline migration would be a better approach.

Whether you choose online or offline migration, data compression is one of a few techniques that can accelerate the process. Data compression reduces the number of bits required to represent data, so more data can move using the same network bandwidth or less physical storage media. In addition, enterprises can transfer the most important data -- such as data that powers mission-critical workloads -- first to streamline the online migration. This technique enables users to take advantage of the cloud more quickly, even if the overall migration takes a while. Scanning data to remove redundant or unnecessary files prior to migration can also reduce the total amount of data to be migrated and speed the migration process.

Some popular native and third-party online migration tools includes AWS Server Migration Service, Azure Migrate, Google Cloud Migrate to Virtual Machines, Carbonite Migrate, PlateSpin Migrate, Rsync

Chapter 13:
Introduction to Data Mesh:

Analytics and Machine Learning promise to be the new source of value and strategic differentiation in the market. Most companies however, continue to find it hard to derive adequate value from their data and the challenge of supplying analytics with relevant, high-quality and timely data has remained unsolved for over a decade.

Data Mesh and other architectural patterns have emerged to solve this and hold promise. Data mesh is fundamentally about putting more of the data into the hands of domain experts who understand the data, instead of completely relying on a single data platform team to clean, process, combine and summarize data for every domain team. There is clear business value to be derived from this change (described in the following sections), but the move in this direction involves organizational and technical changes.

The leaders of companies are the experts in navigating their organization, so we'll focus on the technological pieces that enable this change. Data mesh is described well as a high-level concept by Zhamak Dehghani in her blogs on Thoughtworks and her book Data Mesh. One should read this for a high-level understanding of the concept.

The **data mesh architecture** can turbo charger for analytics by providing rapid access to fast-growing distributed domain sets.

This approach eliminates the challenges of **data accessibility** and **availability** at scale. For example, a central ETL pipeline can slow down when data teams have to run several transformations at once. Since business users depend on technologists (engineers and scientists) to get access to data and extract value from it, the data team deals with a lot of pressure. In such scenarios, the data team is largely operational — running around meeting demands that keep piling up.

Before detailing about Data Mesh Architecture, we must understand the falls of monolithic approach.

13.1 Architectural failure modes of Monolithic approach :

Data platform architecture looks like Figure 13.1 below; a centralized piece of architecture whose goal is to:

Ingest data from all corners of the enterprise, ranging from operational and transactional systems and domains that run the business, or external data providers that augment the knowledge of the enterprise. For example, in a media streaming business, data platform is responsible for ingesting large variety of data: the 'media players performance', how their 'users interact with the players', 'songs they play', 'artists they follow', as well as 'labels and artists' that the business has onboarded, the 'financial transactions' with the artists, and external market research data such as 'customer demographic' information.

Cleanse, enrich, and transform the source data into trustworthy data that can address the needs of a diverse set of consumers. In our example, one of the transformations turns the click streams of user interaction to meaningful sessions enriched with details of the user. This attempts to reconstruct the journey and behavior of the user into aggregate views.

Serve the datasets to a variety of consumers with a diverse set of needs. This ranges from analytical consumption to exploring the data looking for insights, machine learning based decision making, to business intelligence reports that summarize the performance of the business. In our media streaming example, the platform can serve near real-time error and quality information about the media players around the globe through distributed log interfaces such as Kafka or serve the static aggregate views of a particular artist's records being played to drive financial payments calculation to the artists and labels.

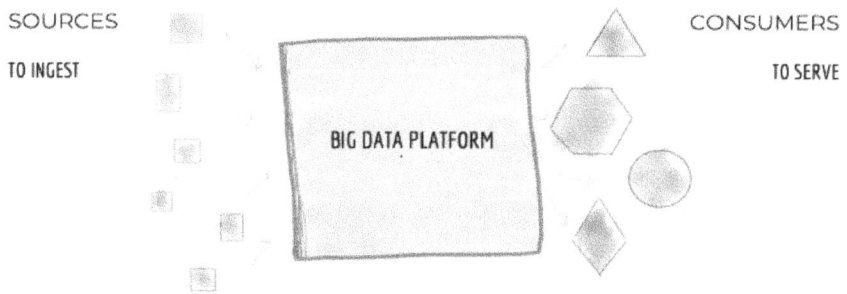

Fig 13.1 - Monolithic Data Platform

It's an accepted convention that the monolithic data platform hosts and owns the data that logically belong to different domains, e.g. 'play events', 'sales KPIs', 'artists', 'albums', 'labels', 'audio', 'podcasts', 'music events', etc.; data from a large number of disparate domains.

While over the last decade we have successfully applied domain driven design and bounded context to our operational systems, we have largely disregarded the domain concepts in a data platform. We have moved away from domain oriented data ownership to a centralized domain agnostic data ownership. We pride ourselves on creating the biggest monolith of them all, the big data platform.

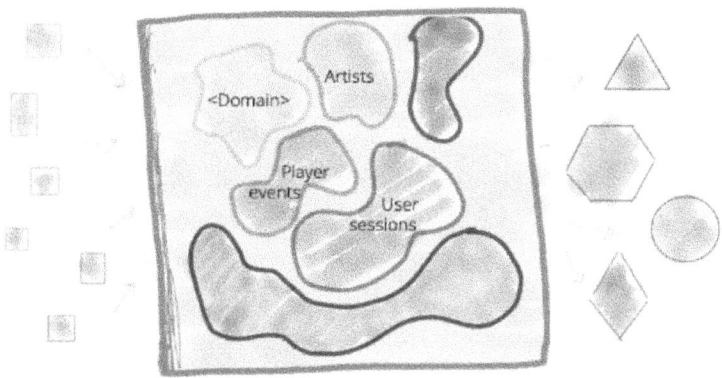

Fig 13.2: Centralized Platform with no clear Data Domain and ownership of domain oriented data

While this centralized model can work for organizations that have a simpler domain with smaller number of diverse consumption cases, it fails for enterprises with rich domains, a large number of sources and a diverse set of consumers.

There are two pressure points on the architecture and the organizational structure of a centralized data platform that often lead to its failure:

- Ubiquitous data and source proliferation: As more data becomes ubiquitously available, the ability to consume it all and harmonize it in one place under the control of one platform diminishes. Imagine just in the domain of 'customer information', there are an increasing number of sources inside and outside of the boundaries of the organization that provide information about the existing and potential customers. The assumption that we need to ingest and store the data in one place to get value from a diverse set of sources is going to constrain our ability to respond to proliferation of data sources. I recognize the need for data users such as data scientists and analysts to process a diverse set of datasets with low overhead, as well as the need to separate the operational systems data usage from the data that is consumed for analytical purposes. But I propose that the existing centralized solution is not the optimal answer for large enterprises with rich domains and continuously adding new sources.

- Organizations' innovation agenda and consumer proliferation: Organizations' need for rapid experimentation introduces a larger number of use cases for consumption of the data from the platform. This implies an ever growing number of transformations on the data - aggregates, projections and slices that can satisfy the test and learn cycle of innovation. The long response time to satisfy the data consumer needs has historically been a point of organizational friction and remains to be so in the modern data platform architecture.

13.2 Coupled pipeline decomposition:

Given the influence of previous generations of data platforms' architecture, architects decompose the data platform to a pipeline of data processing stages. A pipeline that at a very high level implements a functional cohesion around the technical implementation of processing data; i.e. capabilities of ingestion, preparation, aggregation, serving, etc.

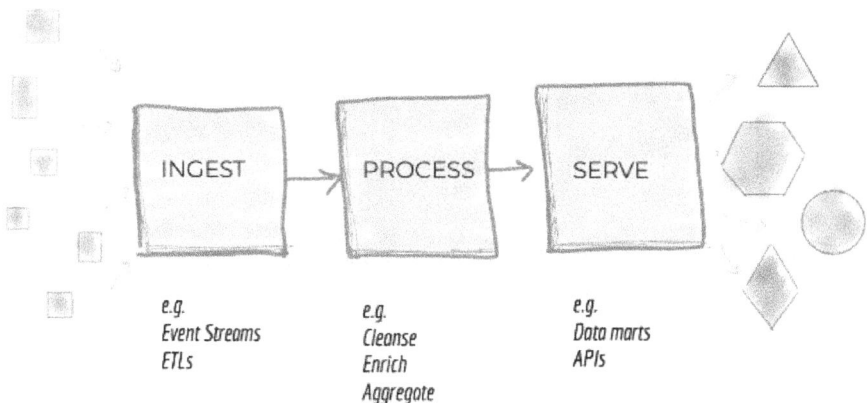

Fig 13.3: Some respite in decomposition of DataPlatform

Though this model provides some level of scale, by assigning teams to different stages of the pipeline, it has an inherent limitation that slows the delivery of features. I will be talking now more on the principles and approach of Data Mesh Architecture

Detailed on Data Mesh :

The data mesh architecture puts the onus of extracting value from data on the data product owner, which frees up the technologists to pursue strategic tasks that enhance the value of data for the entire organization.

Moreover, it facilitates data democratization, empowering every data consumer — data scientists, analysts, business managers — to access, analyze and gain business insights from any data source, without needing help from data engineers.

Now let's look at the guiding principles behind a data mesh architecture. I will focus on an interpretation that is much closer to the ground - a nuts and bolts approach that can be implemented in a few months.

Core principles of a data mesh architecture

According to Dehghani, there are **four principles** that any data mesh setup should embody:

1. Domain-oriented decentralized data ownership and architecture

2. Data as a product

3. Self-serve data infrastructure as a platform

4. Federated computational governance

1. Data Ownership

The goal of the data mesh is to decentralize the entire data ecosystem. Achieving this requires delegating the responsibility of managing data to the folks who work closely with it, i.e., the **data product owners**. This makes it easier to keep the data updated and rapidly incorporate changes.

2. Data as a product

Additionally, to simplify the discovery, understanding, and trustworthiness of data, the data mesh architecture employs the **data-as-a-product principle**. In this principle, the domain-specific data is a "product", and its users are its "customers".

Referring to our previous example, the product would be **Sales** data. The customers would be the scientists, analysts, and sales managers who use sales data for reporting, tracking their metrics, and deriving business insights. For Example:

Let's consider insurance claims. People responsible for building the operational domains that deal with claims are also responsible for providing claims information as easily consumable, trustworthy data, whether as events or, you know, historical snapshots, to the rest of the organization

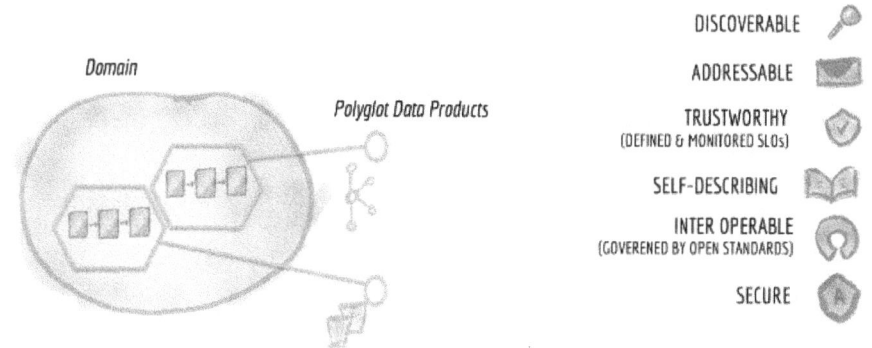

Fig 13.4: Characteristic of domain dataset as product

13.3 Discoverable for Product

A data product must be easily discoverable. A common implementation is to have a registry, a data catalog, of all available data products with their meta information such as their owners, source of origin, lineage, sample datasets, etc. This centralized discoverability service allows data consumers, engineers and scientists in an organization, to find a dataset of their interest easily. Each domain data product must register itself with this centralized data catalog for easy discoverability.

Note the perspective shift here is from a single platform extracting and owning the data for its use, to each domain providing its data as a product in a discoverable fashion.

Addressable

A data product, once discovered, should have a unique address following a global convention that helps its users to programmatically access it. Organizations may adopt different naming conventions for their data, depending on the underlying storage and format of the data. Considering the ease of use as an objective, in a decentralized architecture, it is necessary for common conventions to be developed. Different domains might store and serve their datasets in different formats, events might be stored and accessed through streams such as Kafka topics, columnar datasets might use CSV files, or AWS S3 buckets of serialized Parquet files. A standard for addressability of datasets in a polyglot environment removes friction when finding and accessing information.

Trustworthy and truthful

No one will use a product that they can't trust. In the traditional data platforms it's acceptable to extract and onboard data that has errors, does not reflect the truth of the business and simply can't be trusted. This is where the majority of the efforts of centralized data pipelines are concentrated, cleansing data after ingestion.

A fundamental shift requires the owners of the data products to provide an acceptable Service Level Objective around the truthfulness of the data, and how closely it reflects the reality of the events that have occurred or the high probability of the truthfulness of the insights that have been generated. Applying data cleansing and automated data integrity testing at the point of creation of the data product are some of the techniques to be utilized to provide an acceptable level of quality. Providing data provenance and data lineage as the metadata associated with each data product helps consumers gain further confidence in the data product and its suitability for their particular needs.

The target value or range of a data integrity (quality) indicator varies between domain data products. For example, 'play event' domain may provide two different data products, one near-real-time with lower level of accuracy, including missing or duplicate events, and one with longer delay and higher level of events accuracy. Each data product defines and assures the target level of its integrity and truthfulness as a set of SLOs.

Self-describing semantics and syntax

Quality products require no consumer hand holding to be used: they can be independently discovered, understood and consumed. Building datasets as products with minimum friction for the data engineers and data scientists to use requires well described semantics and syntax of the data, ideally accompanied with sample datasets as examples. Data schemas are a starting point to provide self-serve data assets.

Inter-operable and governed by global standards

One of the main concerns in a distributed domain data architecture, is the ability to correlate data across domains and stitch them together in wonderful, insightful ways; join, filter, aggregate, etc. The key for an effective correlation of data across domains is following certain standards and harmonization rules. Such standardizations should belong to a global governance, to enable interoperability between polyglot domain datasets. Common concerns of such standardization efforts are field type formatting, identifying polysemy across different domains, datasets address conventions, common metadata fields, event formats such as CloudEvents, etc.

For example, in the media streaming business, an 'artist' might appear in different domains and have different attributes and identifiers in each domain. The 'play eventstream' domain may recognize the artist differently to 'artists payment' domain that takes care of invoices and payments. However, to be able to correlate the data about an artist across different domain data products we need to agree on how we identify an artist as a polysemy. One approach is to consider 'artist' with a federated entity and a unique global federated entity identifier for the 'artist', similarly to how federated identities are managed.

Interoperability and standardization of communications, governed globally, is one of the foundational pillars for building distributed systems.

Secure and governed by a global access control

Accessing product datasets securely is a must, whether the architecture is centralized or not. In the world of decentralized domain- oriented data products, the access control is applied at a finer granularity, for each domain data product. Similarly, to operational domains the access control policies can be defined centrally but applied at the time of access to each individual dataset product. Using the Enterprise Identity Management system (SSO) and Role Based Access Control policy definition is a convenient way to implement product datasets access control.

Section Data and self-service platform design convergence describes the shared infrastructure that enables the above capabilities for each data product easily and automatically.

Domain data cross-functional teams

Domains that provide data as products need to be augmented with new skill sets: (a) the data product owner and (b) data engineers.

A data product owner makes decisions around the vision and the roadmap for the data products, concerns herself with the satisfaction of her consumers and continuously measures and improves the quality and richness of the data her domain owns and produces. She is responsible for the lifecycle of the domain datasets, when to change, revise and retire data and schemas. She strikes a balance between the competing needs of the domain data consumers.

Data product owners must define success criteria and business-aligned Key Performance Indicators (KPIs) for their data products. For example, the lead time for consumers of a data product to discover and use the data product successfully, is a measurable success criterion.

In order to build and operate the internal data pipelines of the domains, teams must include data engineers. A wonderful side effect of such a cross-functional team is cross pollination of different skills. My current industry observation is that some data engineers, while competent in using the tools of their trade, lack software engineering standard practices, such as continuous delivery and automated testing, when it comes to building data assets. Similarly, software engineers who are building operational systems often have no experience utilizing data engineering tool sets. Removing the skillset silos will lead to creation of a larger and deeper pool of data engineering skill sets available to the organization. We have observed the same cross-skill pollination with the DevOps movement, and the birth of new types of engineers such as SREs.

Data must be treated as a foundational piece of any software ecosystem; hence software engineers and software generalists must add the experience and knowledge of data product development to their tool belt. Similarly, infrastructure engineers need to add knowledge and experience of managing a data infrastructure. Organizations must provide career development pathways from a generalist to a data engineer. The lack of data engineering skills has led to the local optimization of forming centralized data engineering teams as described in section Siloed and hyper-specialized ownership.

13.4 Self-serve data platform:

It must also be easy to put the data pipelines into production (possibly using templates provided by the data platform team) to keep the datasets updated on a regular cadence. The datasets that are designed to be used by other teams (or are ready to be used by other members of the same team for analytics) should be published explicitly. How does the user evaluate if this dataset is right for them? The user should be able to find and visit the dataset page and evaluate the fitness of these datasets

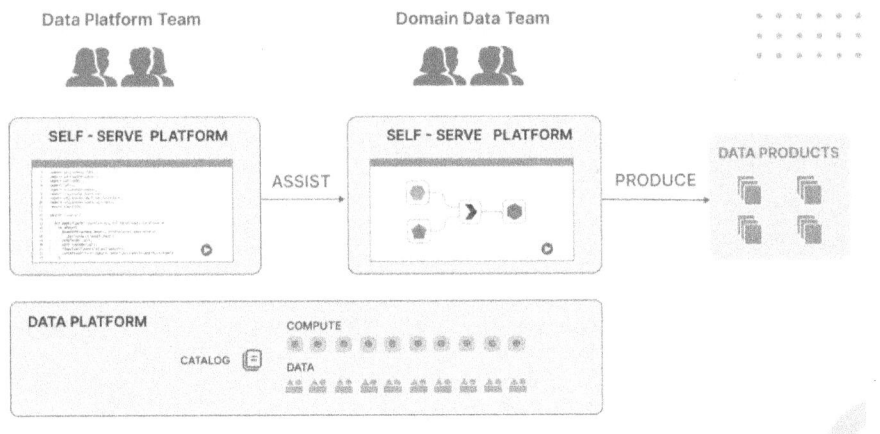

Fig 13.5: Self Service platform for Domain data

The data mesh should be supported by a self-serve infrastructure to make data democratization a reality and make it easy to set up and run different data domains.

Such a platform allows all data owners set up polyglot storage (i.e., various forms of storing data) and helps them provide access to these domains securely. Moreover, the setup shouldn't require any complex engineering skills or support from technologists. To make analytical data product development accessible to generalists, the self-serve platform should support any domain data product developer. It should lower the cost and specialization needed to build data products.

4. Federated computational governance

The **data mesh** concept champions a federated computational governance model for seamless **interoperability**. However, the data shouldn't live in silos despite having a decentralized architecture.

Instead, the entire data ecosystem must be interoperable to extract meaning from data. That's because everything from finding patterns to performing transformations requires all the data products to talk to each other. Lastly, it should follow the standards set by an organization's data governance program to avoid security and compliance-related issues. It must embrace decentralization and domain self-sovereignty, interoperability through global standardization, dynamic topology, and automated execution of decisions by the platform.

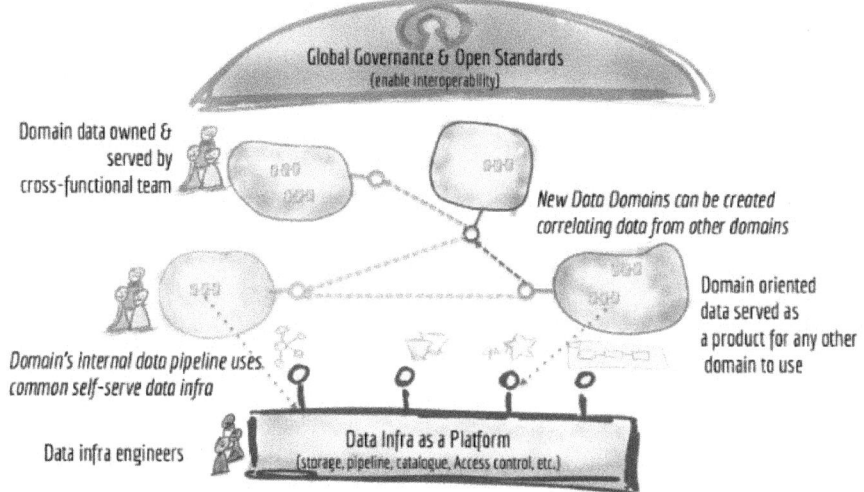

Fig 13.6: High level Data Mesh distribution

Chapter 14
Data Security:

The data economy presents lucrative opportunities for novel business models, with data security emerging as a paramount concern across various sectors such as banking, financial institutions (FIs), and non-banking financial companies (NBFCs).

14.1 What is Data Security?

Data security involves safeguarding corporate and government data, preventing unauthorized access and data loss. It encompasses protection against threats like ransomware and data tampering. Ensuring data availability within the organization is also a key aspect. The rise in cyber-attacks has fueled the need for scalable data security solutions. Cybercriminals employ various malicious tactics to breach networks, often targeting endpoints, data, and cloud environments. Their goal is to steal critical business and consumer data, causing disruptions and losses in intellectual property, finances, and sensitive customer information such as personally identifiable information (PII) and sensitive personal data or information (SPDI), resulting in security breaches and identity theft.

Certain sectors demand stringent data security to adhere to data protection rules. For instance, entities handling payment card details need to securely handle and store this information. Similarly, healthcare organizations in the USA must ensure the secure handling of private health information (PHI) as per the HIPAA standard.

Even without regulatory mandates, the viability of a contemporary business hinges on data security, affecting both organizational assets and customer's private data.

Legal actions, financial settlements, and penalties linked to data breaches are increasing. Numerous governments are implementing stricter data privacy regulations. Consumers possess broader rights, particularly in the EU, California, and Australia, due to the advent of GDPR, CCPA, APP, and CSP234.

Businesses in regulated sectors must comply with extra standards, like HIPAA for US healthcare firms and PCI/DSS for those handling credit card data.

14.2 Classification of Data Security :

- ✓ Cyber-attacks and hacking ✓ Ransomware ✓ Insider threats
- ✓ Data Breaches ✓ Third party risk ✓ Cloud and Api Security

Data Security vs Data Privacy

Data privacy involves categorizing data in a computer system as either shareable with third parties (non-private data) or not shareable (private data). Enforcing data privacy centers on two main aspects.

Access control— Verification of identity and authorization to access specific data are key in ensuring that those attempting to access the data are authenticated and allowed access only to authorized information.

Data protection— Data protection measures guarantee that unauthorized access to data does not allow viewing or damage. These methods involve encryption, rendering data unreadable without the private encryption key, and data loss prevention mechanisms to restrict sensitive data transfer outside the organization.

Data security and data privacy share many elements, with similar mechanisms in place. However, their main distinction lies in their focus: data privacy emphasizes confidentiality, whereas data security prioritizes protection against malicious actions. Encryption, while effective for privacy, may not be enough for security, as attackers could still cause harm by deleting or double-encrypting data.

14.3 Data Security Risks

Below are several common issues faced by organizations of all sizes as they attempt to secure sensitive data.

Accidental Exposure

Many data breaches stem from inadvertent or careless actions rather than intentional attacks. Employees in organizations often unintentionally share, grant access to, or mishandle sensitive data due to a lack of awareness about security policies. Addressing this issue requires employee training and implementing measures like data loss prevention (DLP) technology and enhanced access controls.

Phishing and Other Social Engineering Attacks

Attackers often use social engineering as a key tactic to acquire sensitive data. This involves manipulating individuals into divulging private information or granting access to privileged accounts. Phishing, a prevalent form of social engineering, utilizes deceptive messages appearing to be from trusted sources, ultimately sent by the attacker. When victims fall for this and provide private information or click on malicious links, it opens the door for attackers to compromise their devices or infiltrate corporate networks.

Insider Threats

Insider threats are employees who inadvertently or intentionally threaten the security of an organization's data. There are three types of insider threats:

Non-malicious insider—these are users that can cause harm accidentally, via negligence, or because they are unaware of security procedures.

Malicious insider—these are users who actively attempt to steal data or cause harm to the organization for personal gain.

Compromised insider—these are users who are not aware that their accounts or credentials were compromised by an external attacker. The attacker can then perform malicious activity, pretending to be a legitimate user.

Ransomware

Ransomware poses a significant threat to data across companies of varying sizes. It's a type of malware that infiltrates corporate devices, encrypting data and rendering it useless without a decryption key. Attackers demand payment in exchange for the key, but even if paid, data recovery is often unsuccessful. Various strains of ransomware can swiftly spread and affect extensive portions of a corporate network. If an organization lacks up-to-date backups or if the ransomware compromises backup servers, recovery options may be limited or non-existent.

SQL Injection

SQL injection (SQLi) is a prevalent method used by attackers to illegitimately access databases, pilfer data, and execute unauthorized actions. This technique involves inserting malicious code into what appears to be a harmless database query.

By incorporating special characters into user input, SQL injection alters the query's context, causing the database to inadvertently process harmful code that aligns with the attacker's objectives. SQL injection exposes critical data like customer records and intellectual property, potentially granting attackers administrative database access, leading to severe consequences. Typically, SQL injection vulnerabilities arise from insecure coding practices. Employing secure mechanisms to handle user inputs, readily available in modern database systems, can effectively thwart SQL injection.

14.4 Common Data Security Solutions and Techniques

There are several technologies and practices that can improve data security. No one technique can solve the problem, but by combining several of the techniques below, organizations can significantly improve their security posture.

Data Discovery and Classification

Modern IT environments store data on servers, endpoints, and cloud systems. Visibility over data flows is an important first step in understanding what data is at risk of being stolen or misused. To properly protect your data, you need to know the type of data, where it is, and what it is used for. Data discovery and classification tools can help.

Data detection is the basis for knowing what data you have. Data classification allows you to create scalable security solutions, by identifying which data is sensitive and needs to be secured. Data detection and classification solutions enable tagging files on endpoints, file servers, and cloud storage systems, letting you visualize data across the enterprise, to apply the appropriate security policies.

Data Masking

Data masking allows for the generation of a synthetic rendition of organizational data, suitable for tasks like software testing and training, where real data isn't necessary. The objective is to safeguard data while offering a practical substitute when required. Data masking preserves data types while altering values, achieved through methods like encryption, character rearrangement, or character/word substitution. Regardless of the chosen method, the values must be transformed in a manner that prevents reverse engineering.

Identity Access Management

Identity and Access Management (IAM) constitutes a business approach, strategy, and technological structure facilitating the administration of digital identities within organizations. IAM solutions empower IT administrators to regulate user access to sensitive data within the organization.

Systems used for IAM include single sign-on systems, two-factor authentication, multi-factor authentication, and privileged access management. These technologies enable the organization to securely store identity and profile data, and support governance, ensuring that the appropriate access policies are applied to each part of the infrastructure.

Data Encryption

Data encryption is a method of converting data from a readable format (plaintext) to an unreadable encoded format (ciphertext). Only after decrypting the encrypted data using the decryption key, the data can be read or processed.

In public-key cryptography techniques, there is no need to share the decryption key – the sender and recipient each have their own key, which are combined to perform the encryption operation. This is inherently more secure.

Data encryption can prevent hackers from accessing sensitive information. It is essential for most security strategies and is explicitly required by many compliance standards.

Data Loss Prevention (DLP)

To prevent data loss, organizations can use a number of safeguards, including backing up data to another location. Physical redundancy can help protect data from natural disasters, outages, or attacks on local servers. Redundancy can be performed within a local data center, or by replicating data to a remote site or cloud environment.

Beyond basic measures like backup, DLP software solutions can help protect organizational data. DLP software automatically analyzes content to identify sensitive data, enabling central control and enforcement of data protection policies, and alerting in real-time when it detects anomalous use of sensitive data, for example, large quantities of data copied outside the corporate network.

Password Hygiene

A fundamental data security best practice involves ensuring users utilize strong, unique passwords. Without centralized control, users often resort to easily guessable passwords or use the same password across various services, making them susceptible to password spraying and brute force attacks. Implementing longer passwords and frequent password changes is a basic step.

However, organizations should go beyond this by considering multi-factor authentication (MFA) solutions. MFA necessitates users to authenticate using a token device, or biometrics. Additionally, employing an enterprise password manager, which securely stores encrypted employee passwords, can alleviate the challenge of managing multiple passwords for various corporate systems, although it introduces its own security risks.

Authentication and Authorization

Organizations must put in place strong authentication methods, such as OAuth for web-based systems. It is highly recommended to enforce multi-factor authentication when any user, whether internal or external, requests sensitive or personal data.

In addition, organizations must have a clear authorization framework in place, which ensures that each user has exactly the access rights they need to perform a function or consume a service, and no more. Periodic reviews and automated tools should be used to clean up permissions and remove authorization for users who no longer need them.

Data Security Audits

The organization should perform security audits at least every few months. This identifies gaps and vulnerabilities across the organizations' security posture. It is a good idea to perform the audit via a third-party expert, for example in a penetration testing model. However, it is also possible to perform a security audit in house. Most importantly, when the audit exposes security issues, the organization must devote time and resources to address and remediate them.

Anti-Malware, Antivirus, and Endpoint Protection

Malware is the most common vector of modern cyberattacks, so organizations must ensure that endpoints like employee workstations, mobile devices, servers, and cloud systems, have appropriate protection. The basic measure is antivirus software, but this is no longer enough to address new threats like file-less attacks and unknown zero-day malware.

Endpoint protection platforms (EPP) take a more comprehensive approach to endpoint security. They combine antivirus with a machine-learning-based analysis of anomalous behavior on the device, which can help detect unknown attacks. Most platforms also provide endpoint detection and response (EDR) capabilities, which help security teams identify breaches on endpoints as they happen, investigate them, and respond by locking down and reimaging affected endpoints.

Zero Trust Architecture

Zero trust is a security model introduced by Forrester analyst John Kindervag, which has been adopted by the US government, several technical standards bodies, and many of the world's largest technology companies. The basic principle of zero trust is that no entity on a network should be trusted, regardless of whether it is outside or inside the network perimeter but must verify

Zero trust has a special focus on data security, because data is the primary asset attackers are interested in. A zero trust architecture aims to protect data against insider and outside threats by continuously verifying all access attempts, and denying access by default.

Zero trust security mechanisms build multiple security layers around sensitive data—for example, they use micro segmentation to ensure sensitive assets on the network are isolated from other assets. In a true zero trust network, attackers have very limited access to sensitive data, and there are controls that can help detect and respond to any anomalous access to data.

Penetration Testing

Penetration testing, also known as pen testing, is a method of evaluating the security of a computer system or network by simulating an attack on it. The goal of pen testing is to identify vulnerabilities in the system that an attacker could exploit, and to determine the effectiveness of the system's defenses against these vulnerabilities.

Penetration testers use a variety of tools and techniques to test the security of a system. These may include network scanners, vulnerability scanners, and other specialized software tools. They may also use manual methods such as social engineering or physical access to the system.

Penetration testing is an important part of an organization's overall security strategy. It helps organizations identify and fix vulnerabilities before they can be exploited by malicious actors, and it can help organizations improve their defenses against future attacks.

Database Security

Database security involves protecting database management systems such as Oracle, SQL Server, or MySQL, from unauthorized use and malicious cyber attacks. The main elements protected by database security are:

The database management system (DBMS). Data stored in the database, Applications associated with the DBMS, The physical or virtual database server and any underlying hardware. Any computing and network infrastructure used to access the database.

A database security strategy involves tools, processes, and methodologies to securely configure and maintain security inside a database environment and protect databases from intrusion, misuse, and damage.

Technical standards bodies have recommended email security protocols including SSL/TLS, Sender Policy Framework (SPF), and DomainKeys Identified Mail (DKIM). These protocols are implemented by email clients and servers, including Microsoft Exchange and Google G Suite, to ensure secure delivery of emails. A secure email gateway helps organizations and individuals protect their email from a variety of threats, in addition to implementing security protocols.

14.4 Best Data Security Tips:

In word of George Washington "The best defense is best offence" and thus we look at key practice like protecting, auditing, managing, updating and encrypting the data. Given that additional practice can be placed for unauthorized access such as :

Sl No	Description	Sl No	Description
1	Understanding Data, Database, Technologies	2	Practicing Data Identification, Classification, Access Control and Data Usage
3	Masking the critical Demo Graphic Data	4	Implementation Change Management and Database auditing
5	Backing your Data	6	Rapid Configuration or Data Storage with encryption and Audit tools
7	Patch Management and System hardening	8	Insider threat Management like securing remote access
9	Negative, Zero and Positive Trust	10	Managing Camera based Malware
11	Wearable risk surface and hackable E- waste	11	The death of Personal Password
12	Cloud Camouflage should be confronted	13	Personal data Loss Tsunami
13	Importance of GDPR, DPDP And CCPA	14	Certification from authorized audit firm like PCI-DSS, HIPPA, ISO 27001
15	More focus on API Security and attacks	16	More awareness among Employee and Partners

17	Focus on high installation cost, Next generation firewalls (NGFWs)	18	Re treat on advance threat protection (ATP).
19	Enablement of VPN (Virtual Private Network), Notable endpoint, SSL Kill	20	Robust Cyber Hygiene Policies
21	Enablement of use of AI and Threat actors, shooting Cat and Mouse play between Attackers and Defenders	22	Biometric and Behavioral Authentication
23	Data Resiliency from post of Cyber- attacks, ensuring safeguards data by providing immutable, logically air gaped data protection with multi factor authentication-based access control	24	Focus on Data Observability to monitor risks and investigate threats to data including Ransomware monitoring, sensitivities data discovery, threat monitoring and hunting
25	Attention for Data Recovery for quickly contains threat and recover data, be it file, application data or the Mass recovery for the entire organization	26	The financial penalties, obligations and duties of stakeholder

14.5 Indian Digital Personal Data Protection Bill 2023

History:

Personal data refers to information linked to a specific individual. Businesses and government bodies process personal data to provide goods and services, tailoring experiences, targeted advertising, and creating recommendations. This data processing can also assist law enforcement. However, unregulated processing can infringe upon individuals' privacy, recognized as a fundamental right, leading to potential harm like financial loss, reputational damage, and profiling.

As of now, India lacks an independent data protection law. The use of personal data is governed by the Information Technology (IT) Act, 2000. In 2017, the central government formed a Committee of Experts on Data Protection, chaired by Justice B. N. Srikrishna, to address data protection matters. The Committee presented its report in July 2018, leading to the introduction of the Personal Data Protection Bill, 2019 in Lok Sabha in December 2019. Following deliberation by a Joint Parliamentary Committee, a report was submitted in December 2021. However, in August 2022, the Bill was withdrawn from Parliament. Subsequently, in November 2022, a Draft Bill was made available for public input. In August 2023, the Digital Personal Data Protection Bill, 2023 was presented in Parliament.

Key Features

- **Applicability:** The Bill applies to the processing of digital personal data within India where such data is: (i) collected online, or (ii) collected offline and is digitised. It will also apply to the processing of personal data outside India if it is for offering goods or services in India. Personal data is defined as any data about an individual who is identifiable by or in relation to such data. Processing has been defined as wholly or partially automated operation or set of operations performed on digital personal data. It includes collection, storage, use, and sharing.

- **Consent:** Personal data may be processed only for a lawful purpose after obtaining the consent of the individual. A notice must be given before seeking consent. The notice should contain details about the personal data to be collected and the purpose of processing. Consent may be withdrawn at any point in time. Consent will not be required for 'legitimate uses' including: (i) specified purpose for which data has been provided by an individual voluntarily, (ii) provision of benefit or service by the government, (iii) medical emergency, and (iv) employment. For individuals below 18 years of age, consent will be provided by the parent or the legal guardian.

- **Rights and duties of data principal:** An individual whose data is being processed (data principal), will have the right to: (i) obtain information about processing, (ii) seek correction and erasure of personal data, (iii) nominate another person to exercise rights in the event of death or incapacity, and (iv) grievance redressal. Data principals will have certain duties. They must not: (i) register a false or frivolous complaint, and (ii) furnish any false particulars or impersonate another person in specified cases. Violation of duties will be punishable with a penalty of up to Rs 10,000.

- **Obligations of data fiduciaries:** The entity determining the purpose and means of processing, (data fiduciary), must: (i) make reasonable efforts to ensure the accuracy and completeness of data, (ii) build reasonable security safeguards to prevent a data breach, (iii) inform the Data Protection Board of India and affected persons in the event of a breach, and (iv) erase personal data as soon as the purpose has been met and retention is not necessary for legal purposes (storage limitation). In case of government entities, storage limitation and the right of the data principal to erasure will not apply.

- **Transfer of personal data outside India:** The Bill allows transfer of personal data outside India, except to countries restricted by the central government through notification.

- **Exemptions:** Rights of the data principal and obligations of data fiduciaries (except data security) will not apply in specified cases. These include: (i) prevention and investigation of offences, and (ii) enforcement of legal rights or claims. The central government may, by notification, exempt certain activities from the application of the Bill. These include: (i) processing by government entities in the interest of the security of the state and public order, and (ii) research, archiving, or statistical purposes.

- **Data Protection Board of India:** The central government will establish the Data Protection Board of India. Key functions of the Board include: (i) monitoring compliance and imposing penalties, (ii) directing data fiduciaries to take necessary measures in the event of a data breach, and (iii) hearing grievances made by affected persons. Board members will be appointed for two years and will be eligible for re-appointment. The central government will prescribe details such as the number of members of the Board and the selection process. Appeals against the decisions of the Board will lie with TDSAT.

- **Penalties:** The schedule to the Bill specifies penalties for various offences such as up to: (i) Rs 200 crore for non-fulfillment of obligations for children, and (ii) Rs 250 crore for failure to take security measures to prevent data breaches. Penalties will be imposed by the Board after conducting an inquiry.

- Various technology platform for Bank is under discussion to find how the technology component need to be placed to capture the consent and how it will be integrated with many channels. For consent deletion, technical platform like Salesforce Platform where Many Api Service will be used, other alternative option is MDM which can hold Demographic data point and be potential platform.

- Consent for Case of Death, for Minor, how the Nomination can transfer and ownership so that it will help the citizen along with FIs. The challenge in both of cases is technical as well as process and governance on how to implement it. because Most of Consent cases has to attached to CBS (Core banking system) and it needs hollowing the CBS System as well which is very complex environment for Banks.

14.6 Summary of Third Generation

While we have been addressing numerous infrastructure challenges with the adoption of cloud solutions, focusing on scalability, we have also witnessed the emergence of new technologies such as Kubernetes and Docker for efficient infrastructure management. The Data Cloud platform, on the other hand, is geared towards resolving long-standing issues related to real-time or near-real-time data acquisition from various sources, including different data formats like files, structured, unstructured, social data, videos, and images. These data operations serve as versatile tools for AI/ML feature engineering, modeling, and deployment.

Additionally, the platform ensures seamless access to centralized datasets for users. This becomes particularly valuable when self-service teams are tasked with building extensive reporting and analytics using a range of BI tools like Power BI and Tableau. Users often require data discovery, exploratory analytics, and the ability to create data science models using the modernized tools available in the cloud.

We also got to know the When the data required at the beginning of your analysis, Why you need data driven decisions require well organize data, What are techniques are required for Data ingestion, preprocessing, Data cleansing, Where the data comes from like Customer data, Historical data, Social data, Financial data, Medical records data, How using what tools of Cloud like Azure Synapsis , Databricks, adls, Cosmodb, Purview ,Similarly AWS bunch of tool like S3,Dynamodb , Lamda, Cloud HSM etc, GCP bigquery, Datafusion etc and lastly Who are the key players like Data Engineer, Data Analysts ,DS do the core work in the Cloud. We also saw the various migration techniques from on prem to cloud with Various frameworks and options for history data load, delta load etc. We also saw the Data mash concept that helps in bringing Data Domain and self Service to the Data where data can be monetized quickly. Account Aggregator (AAs) is the new innovative Platform for the customer benefit and transparent in the banking space.

Effective decision-making involves a harmonious blend of data analysis, human judgment, and the input of various stakeholders. It is imperative to solicit insights from diverse groups, including subject matter experts, data analysts, business leaders, and front-line employees who have direct customer interactions. A recent survey of over 3,000 CEOs worldwide emphasized the significance of data in decision-making, advocating that we should leverage data as a tool to inform our decisions rather than the other way around. To achieve this, a wide array of planning approaches should be employed, such as forecasting, modeling, scenario-based planning, benchmarking, and datamining.

Recognizing that a one-size-fits-all decision-making model is insufficient for all scenarios is essential. Thus, reliance on the expertise of a Chief Data Officer (CDO) is pivotal for decisions regarding data and cybersecurity. The CDO plays a crucial role in areas like data management, data reliability, regulatory compliance, data ownership, and data integration. Additionally, collaboration with the Chief Sustainability Officer (CSO) and Chief Financial Officer (CFO) is vital to develop a balanced sustainability and profitability roadmap based on data-driven insights.

CEOs today draw from a multitude of information sources when making strategic decisions. The growing volume of data, including emerging areas like Environmental, Social, and Governance (ESG) data, alongside increasing external inputs, makes decision-making more complex than ever before.

An illustrative example of this evolving landscape is the recent Global Fintech Fest (GFF) held in Mumbai on September 7th, 2023, where over 500 fintech companies showcased innovative products for the banking sector. The event underscored the pivotal role of Digital Public Infrastructure in fostering innovation, a theme supported by many countries. This platform, facilitated by fintech advancements, has made processes faster, more reliable, and easily accessible through the banking system.

Global fintech has already generated $245 billion as of today and is projected to reach $1.5 trillion by 2030. India's fintech sector is also poised for remarkable growth, with expectations to generate $200 billion by 2030. Notably, digital transactions in India have surged from 1.2 billion in 2014 to 91 billion in 2022, accompanied by a substantial increase in mobile internet users, from 70 million in 2014 to 800 million in 2022. Realizing the potential of this landscape requires the integration of data, cloud computing, AI, and microservice architecture to create a robust and scalable public digital platform.

So far , our relentless pursuit of enhancing Data Platforms, optimizing Data Processing, and exploring diverse use cases for Monetization, we find ourselves facing a paradox: the imperative to safeguard our data. In the current digital age, the state of privacy appears dismal, and regrettably, it seems poised to deteriorate further. Thus, the responsibility to protect our data falls squarely upon our shoulders. Data security is not merely a technical concern; it has evolved into a trust currency crucial to navigating the digital landscape.

In an era where vast volumes of data float freely in the online realm, it is a clarion call for individuals to grasp the inherent worth of their personal data. As we openly share our lives and thoughts in the digital sphere, it becomes paramount to accord our data the same meticulous care that we reserve for our most prized possessions. Data security extends beyond the boardrooms of corporations; it metamorphoses into a deeply personal responsibility. During our discussions, we delved into various techniques, the pivotal role of governance, and the significance of regulatory bodies in this context.

The sagacious words of Tim Berners-Lee, the visionary behind the World Wide Web, resound with significance: "Data is a precious thing and will last longer than the systems themselves." These words serve as a poignant reminder that data possesses a longevity that outlives the transient technologies and platforms from which it originates. It persists within digital archives, resides on cloud servers, and endures within databases long after the devices that generated it have faded into obsolescence. This enduring quality underscores the critical imperative of diligently safeguarding our data, fortifying it against breaches and unauthorized access.

www.ingramcontent.com/pod-product-compliance
Lightning Source LLC
LaVergne TN
LVHW061544070526
838199LV00077B/6893